Contents

Microsoft® Access® Level 1

Unit 1

Creating Tables and Queries

Microsoft® Access®

Managing and Creating Access Tables

Study Tools

Study tools include a presentation and a list of chapter Quick Steps and Hint margin notes. Use these resources to help you further develop and review skills learned in this chapter.

Concepts Check

Check your understanding by identifying application tools used in this chapter. If you are a SNAP user, launch the Concepts Check from your Assignments page.

Recheck

Check your understanding by taking this quiz. If you are a SNAP user, launch the Recheck from your Assignments page.

Skills Exercise

Additional activities are available to SNAP users. If you are a SNAP user, access these activities from your Assignments page.

Skills Assessment

The database designer for Griffin Technologies has created the database diagram shown in Figure WB-1.1 to manage data about company employees. You will open the Griffin database and maintain and create tables that follow this diagram.

Figure WB-1.1 Griffin Technologies Database Diagram

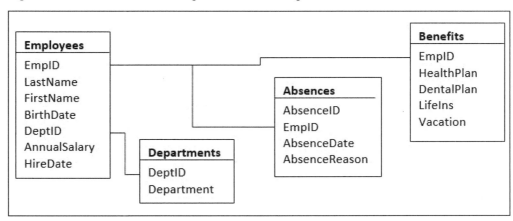

Insert and Delete Rows and Columns

1. In Access, open **1-Griffin.accdb** and enable the content.
2. Double-click *Employees* in the Tables group in the Navigation pane.
3. Delete the record for Scott Jorgensen (employee number 1025).
4. Delete the record for Leanne Taylor (employee number 1060).
5. Add the following records:

EmpID	1010		*EmpID*	1052
LastName	Harrington		*LastName*	Reeves
FirstName	Tyler		*FirstName*	Carrie
BirthDate	9/7/1979		*BirthDate*	12/4/1981
AnnualSalary	$53,350		*AnnualSalary*	$38,550
HireDate	10/1/2013		*HireDate*	10/1/2018

6. Close the Employees table.
7. Looking at the database diagram in Figure WB-1.1, you realize that the Employees table includes a *DeptID* field column. Open the Employees table, insert the new field column in the Employees table, and name it *DeptID*. Change the field size to 2 characters (since department abbreviations are only one or two letters in length). At the message stating that some data may be lost, click Yes. Type the department identification for each record as shown below (the records are listed from left to right):

1001: HR	1002: RD	1003: IT	1005: DP	1010: DP
1013: RD	1015: HR	1020: A	1023: IT	1030: PR
1033: A	1040: DP	1043: HR	1045: RD	1050: IT
1052: PR	1053: HR	1063: DP	1065: DP	1080: IT
1083: HR	1085: PR	1090: RD	1093: A	1095: RD

8. Move the *DeptID* field column so it is positioned between the *BirthDate* field column and the *AnnualSalary* field column.
9. Automatically adjust the widths of the columns.
10. Save the table.
11. Display the table in Print Preview, change the top margin to 1.5 inches, change the left margin to 1.25 inches, and then print the table.
12. Close the Employees table.

Create a Departments Table

1. You entered a one- or two-letter abbreviation representing each department within the company. Creating the abbreviations saved you from having to type the entire department name for each record. You need to create the Departments table that will provide the department name for each abbreviation. Create a new table in the **1-Griffin.accdb** database with the field names and data shown in Figure WB-1.2 by completing the following steps:
   a. Click the Create tab and then click the Table button.
   b. Click the *ID* column heading, click the *Data Type* option box arrow in the Formatting group, and then click *Short Text* at the drop-down list.
   c. Limit the field size to 2 characters and rename the field to *DeptID*.

d. Click *Click to Add*, click *Short Text* at the drop-down list, and then type Department.
e. Type the data in the fields as shown in Figure WB-1.2.
f. Automatically adjust the widths of the columns.
2. Save the table and name it *Departments*.
3. Print and then close the table.

Figure WB-1.2 Departments Table

DeptID ▾	Department	▾	Click to Add ▾
A	Accounting		
DP	Design and Production		
HR	Human Resources		
IT	Information Technology Services		
PR	Public Relations		
RD	Research and Development		
*			

Assessment 3

Create a Benefits Table

1. Create a new table in **1-Griffin.accdb** using the data shown in Figure WB-1.3 and with the following specifications:
   a. Name the fields as shown in the Benefits table in the diagram in Figure WB-1.1 and create the caption names for the fields as shown in Figure WB-1.3. (For example, name the life insurance field *LifeIns* and create the caption *Life Insurance*.)
   b. For the first column, click the *ID* field name, click the *Data Type* option box arrow in the Formatting group, and then click *Short Text* at the drop-down list. Limit the field size to 4 characters and rename the field as *EmpID*.
   c. Apply the Yes/No data type to the second column, make the default value a check mark (by typing Yes at the Expression Builder dialog box), and provide the description *A check mark indicates the employee has signed up for the health plan*.
   d. Apply the Yes/No data type to the third column, make the default value a check mark (by typing Yes at the Expression Builder dialog box), and provide the description *A check mark indicates the employee has signed up for the dental plan*.
   e. Apply the Currency data type to the fourth column.
   f. Apply the Short Text data type to the fifth column and limit the field size to 8 characters.
   g. Type the data in each record as shown in Figure WB-1.3.
   h. Automatically adjust the column widths.
   i. Save the table and name it *Benefits*.
2. Display the table in Print Preview, change the top and left margins to 1.5 inches, and then print the table.
3. Close the Benefits table.

Figure WB-1.3 Benefits Table

EmployeeID	Health Plan	Dental Plan	Life Insurance	Vacation	Click to Add
1030	✓	✓	$100,000.00	4 weeks	
1050	✓	✓	$200,000.00	3 weeks	
1060		✓	$150,000.00	3 weeks	
1090	✓	✓	$200,000.00	3 weeks	
1100	✓	✓	$185,000.00	4 weeks	
1120		✓	$200,000.00	3 weeks	
1170			$100,000.00	3 weeks	
1200	✓	✓	$200,000.00	4 weeks	
1220			$75,000.00	2 weeks	
1250	✓	✓	$125,000.00	3 weeks	
1280	✓	✓	$200,000.00	3 weeks	
1300	✓	✓	$200,000.00	3 weeks	
1320			$50,000.00	2 weeks	
1380	✓		$125,000.00	2 weeks	
1410	✓	✓	$85,000.00	3 weeks	
1430	✓	✓	$175,000.00	3 weeks	
1490	✓		$100,000.00	2 weeks	
1520	✓	✓	$150,000.00	2 weeks	
1530	✓	✓	$200,000.00	2 weeks	
1550		✓	$150,000.00	1 week	
1590	✓		$75,000.00	1 week	
1630	✓	✓	$125,000.00	1 week	
1650	✓		$150,000.00	1 week	
1700		✓	$185,000.00	1 week	
1730	✓	✓	$125,000.00	1 week	
*	✓	✓			

Assessment 4

Sort Data

1. With **1-Griffin.accdb** open, open the Employees table.
2. Using the buttons in the Sort & Filter group on the Home tab determine how to sort columns of data in ascending and descending order.
3. Sort the records in the Employees table in ascending order by last name.
4. Save, print, and then close the Employees table.
5. Open the Benefits table and then sort the records in descending order by life insurance amounts.
6. Save, print, and then close the Benefits table.

Visual Benchmark

Create an Absences Table

1. With **1-Griffin.accdb** open, create the Absences table shown in Figure WB-1.4 (using the field names as shown in Figure WB-1.1) with the following specifications:
   a. Use the default AutoNumber data type for first field column. Apply the appropriate data type to the other field columns.
   b. Create an appropriate caption and description for the *EmpID*, *AbsenceDate*, and *AbsenceReason* columns.
   c. Apply the default value of *Sick Day* to the *AbsenceReason* field column. (You will need to type "Sick Day" in the Expression Builder dialog box.)
2. Save the table and name it *Absences*.
3. Print the table in landscape orientation with top and left margins of 1.5 inches.
4. Close the Absences table and then close **1-Griffin.accdb**.

Figure WB-1.4 Absences Table

AbsenceID	EmpID	Absent Date	Absent Reason	Click to Add
1	1410	1/2/2018	Sick Day	
2	1410	1/5/2018	Sick Day	
3	1050	1/6/2018	Sick Day	
4	1630	1/9/2018	Sick Day	
5	1250	1/9/2018	Bereavement	
6	1250	1/12/2018	Bereavement	
7	1250	1/12/2018	Bereavement	
8	1170	1/13/2018	Sick Day	
9	1700	1/14/2018	Personal Day	
10	1530	1/16/2018	Sick Day	
11	1530	1/19/2018	Sick Day	
12	1030	1/19/2018	Personal Day	
13	1090	1/20/2018	Sick Day	
14	1090	1/22/2018	Sick Day	
15	1670	1/23/2018	Personal Day	
16	1380	1/29/2018	Sick Day	
17	1590	1/30/2018	Sick Day	
* (New)			Sick Day	

Case Study

You are the office manager for Elite Limousines, and your company is switching over to Access for managing company data. The database designer has provided you with the database diagram in Figure WB-1.5. She wants you to follow the diagram when creating the database.

Figure WB-1.5 Elite Limousines Database Diagram

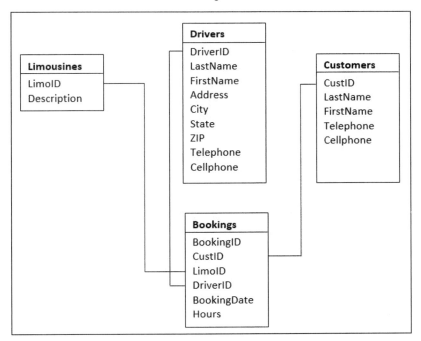

Part 1

Create a new database named **1-Elite.accdb** and then create the Limousines table shown in the database diagram in Figure WB-1.5. The database designer has asked you to include an appropriate caption and description for each field and to change the field size for the *LimoID* field. Type the following records in the table:

LimoID	01		*LimoID*	02
Description	2014 White stretch		*Description*	2014 Black stretch
LimoID	04		*LimoID*	06
Description	2015 Black minibus		*Description*	2015 Black standard
LimoID	08		*LimoID*	10
Description	2017 Black SUV stretch		*Description*	2018 Black stretch

Part 2

With **1-Elite.accdb** open, create the Drivers table shown in the database diagram in Figure WB-1.5. Include appropriate captions and descriptions for each field and change the field sizes where appropriate. Type the following records in the table:

DriverID#	101		*DriverID*	114
LastName	Brennan		*LastName*	Gould
FirstName	Andrea		*FirstName*	Randall
Address	4438 Gowan Rd.		*Address*	330 Aura Ave.
City	Las Vegas		*City*	Las Vegas
State	NV		*State*	NV
ZIP	89115		*ZIP*	89052
Telephone	(702) 555-3481		*Telephone*	(702) 555-1239
Cellphone	(702) 555-1322		*Cellphone*	(702) 555-7474
DriverID	120		*DriverID*	125
LastName	Martinelli		*LastName*	Nunez
FirstName	Albert		*FirstName*	Frank
Address	107 Cameo Dr.		*Address*	4832 Helena St.
City	Las Vegas		*City*	Las Vegas
State	NV		*State*	NV
ZIP	89138		*ZIP*	89129
Telephone	(702) 555-0349		*Telephone*	(702) 555-3748
Cellphone	(702) 555-6649		*Cellphone*	(702) 555-2210

Part 3

With **1-Elite.accdb** open, create the Customers table shown in the database diagram in Figure WB-1.5. Include appropriate captions and descriptions for the fields and change the field sizes where appropriate. Type the following records in the table:

CustID	1001		*CustID*	1002
LastName	Spencer		*LastName*	Tsang
FirstName	Maureen		*FirstName*	Lee
Telephone	(513) 555-3943		*Telephone*	(702) 555-4775
Cellphone	(513) 555-4884		*Cellphone*	(702) 555-4211
CustID	1028		*CustID*	1031
LastName	Gabriel		*LastName*	Marshall
FirstName	Nicholas		*FirstName*	Patricia
Telephone	(612) 555-7885		*Telephone*	(702) 555-6410
Cellphone	(612) 555-7230		*Cellphone*	(702) 555-0137

CustID	1010		CustID	1044
LastName	Chavez		*LastName*	Vanderhage
FirstName	Blake		*FirstName*	Vernon
Telephone	(206) 555-3774		*Telephone*	(213) 555-8846
Cellphone	(206) 555-3006		*Cellphone*	(213) 555-4635

Part 4

With **1-Elite.accdb** open, create the Bookings table shown in the database diagram in Figure WB-1.5. Include appropriate captions and descriptions for the fields and change the field sizes where appropriate. Type the following records in the table:

BookingID	(AutoNumber)		*BookingID*	(AutoNumber)
CustID	1044		*CustID*	1001
LimoID	02		*LimoID*	10
DriverID	114		*DriverID*	120
BookingDate	7/1/2018		*BookingDate*	7/1/2018
Hours	6		*Hours*	8

BookingID	(AutoNumber)		*BookingID*	(AutoNumber)
CustID	1002		*CustID*	1028
LimoID	04		*LimoID*	02
DriverID	101		*DriverID*	125
BookingDate	7/7/2018		*BookingDate*	7/7/2018
Hours	8		*Hours*	4

BookingID	(AutoNumber)		*BookingID*	(AutoNumber)
CustID	1010		*CustID*	1031
LimoID	06		*LimoID*	08
DriverID	125		*DriverID*	120
BookingDate	7/14/2018		*BookingDate*	7/14/2018
Hours	3		*Hours*	5

Automatically adjust the column widths of each table to accommodate the longest entry in each column. Print each table so all records fit on one page.

Creating Relationships between Tables

> **Study Tools**

Study tools include a presentation and a list of chapter Quick Steps and Hint margin notes. Use these resources to help you further develop and review skills learned in this chapter.

> **Concepts Check**

SNAP

Check your understanding by identifying application tools used in this chapter. If you are a SNAP user, launch the Concepts Check from your Assignments page.

> **Recheck**

SNAP

Check your understanding by taking this quiz. If you are a SNAP user, launch the Recheck from your Assignments page.

Skills Exercise

SNAP

Additional activities are available to SNAP users. If you are a SNAP user, access these activities from your Assignments page.

Skills Assessment

The database designer for Copper State Insurance has created the database diagram shown in Figure WB-2.1 to manage company data. You will open the Copper State Insurance database and maintain and create tables that follow this diagram.

Figure WB-2.1 Copper State Insurance Database Design

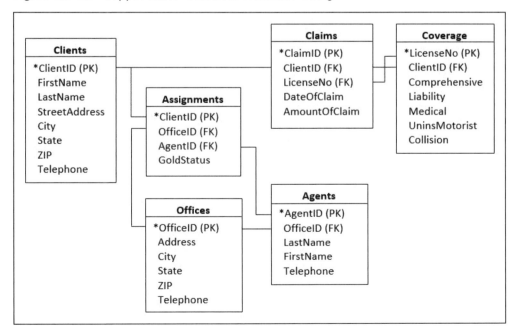

Assessment

1

Create Relationships in an Insurance Company Database

1. Open **2-CopperState.accdb** and enable the content.
2. Open the Claims table.
3. Display the table in Design view, define the *ClaimID* field as the primary key field, click the Save button on the Quick Access Toolbar, and then close the Claims table.
4. Display the Relationships window and then insert the Clients, Claims, and Coverage tables.
5. Create a one-to-many relationship with the *ClientID* field in the Clients table field list box the "one" and the *ClientID* field in the Claims table field list box the "many." Enforce referential integrity and cascade fields and records.
6. Create a one-to-many relationship with the *ClientID* field in the Clients table field list box the "one" and the *ClientID* field in the Coverage table field list box the "many." Enforce referential integrity and cascade fields and records.
7. Create a one-to-many relationship with the *LicenseNo* field in the Coverage table field list box the "one" and the *LicenseNo* field in the Claims table field list box the "many." Enforce referential integrity and cascade fields and records.
8. Save and then print the relationship report.
9. Close the relationship report without saving it and close the Relationships window.

Assessment

2

Create a New Table and Relate the Table

1. With **2-CopperState.accdb** open, create the Offices table shown in Figure WB-2.2. Change the *OfficeID* field column to the Short Text data type. (Do this with the *Data Type* option box in the Formatting group on the Table Tools Fields tab.) Change the field size to 2 characters. Change the default value for the *State* field to *AZ*.
2. After typing the records, adjust the column widths to accommodate the longest entry in each column and then save the Offices table.
3. Print and then close the Offices table.
4. Display the Relationships window and then add the Offices table and the Assignments table to the window.
5. Create a one-to-many relationship with the *OfficeID* field in the Offices table field list box the "one" and the *OfficeID* field in the Assignments table field list box the "many." Enforce referential integrity and cascade fields and records.
6. Create a one-to-one relationship with the *ClientID* field in the Clients table field list box and the *ClientID* field in the Assignments table field list box. Enforce referential integrity and cascade fields and records.
7. Save and then print the relationship report in landscape orientation. To do this, click the Landscape button in the Page Layout group on the Print Preview tab.
8. Close the relationship report without saving it and then close the Relationships window.

Figure WB-2.2 Assessment 2 Offices Table

OfficeID	Address	City	State	ZIP	Telephone	Click to Add
GN	North 51st Avenue	Glendale	AZ	85305	(653) 555-8800	
GW	West Bell Road	Glendale	AZ	85312	(623) 555-4300	
PG	Grant Street West	Phoenix	AZ	85003	(602) 555-6200	
PM	McDowell Road	Phoenix	AZ	85012	(602) 555-3800	
SE	East Thomas Road	Scottsdale	AZ	85251	(480) 555-5500	
SN	North 68th Street	Scottsdale	AZ	85257	(480) 555-9000	
*			AZ			

Assessment

3

Delete and Edit Records in Tables

1. With **2-CopperState.accdb** open, open the Clients table.
2. Delete the record for Harold McDougal (client number 9879). (At the message stating that relationships that specify cascading deletes are about to cause records in this table and related tables to be deleted, click Yes.)
3. Delete the record for Vernon Cook (client number 7335). (At the message stating that relationships that specify cascading deletes are about to cause records in this table and related tables to be deleted, click Yes.)
4. Change the client number for Paul Vuong from *4300* to *2560*.
5. Print the Clients table in landscape orientation and then close the table.
6. Open the Claims table, print the table, and then close the table. (The Claims table initially contained two entries for client number 9879 and one entry for 7335. These entries were deleted automatically when you deleted the records in the Clients table.)

Assessment

4

Display and Edit Records in a Subdatasheet

1. With **2-CopperState.accdb** open, open the Clients table.
2. Click the expand indicator (plus symbol) at the left side of the record for Erin Hagedorn. At the Insert Subdatasheet dialog box, click *Claims* in the list box and then click OK.
3. Change the amount of the claim from *$1,450.00* to *$1,797.00*, change Erin's street address from *4818 Oakes Boulevard* to *763 51st Avenue*, and change her zip code from *85018* to *85014*.
4. Click the collapse indicator (minus symbol) at the left side of the record for Erin Hagedorn.
5. Remove the connection between the Clients and Claims tables by clicking the More button in the Records group on the Home tab, pointing to *Subdatasheet*, and then clicking *Remove*.
6. Click the More button in the Records group, point to *Subdatasheet*, and then click *Subdatasheet*. At the Insert Subdatasheet dialog box, click *Coverage* in the list box and then click OK.
7. Expand all records by clicking the More button, pointing to *Subdatasheet*, and then clicking *Expand All*.
8. Change the telephone number for Claire Azevedo (client number 1379) from *(480) 555-2154* to *(480) 555-2143* and insert check marks in the *Medical* field and the *UninsMotorist* field.
9. Change the last name of Joanne Donnelly (client number 1574) to *Marquez* and remove the check mark from the *Collision* field.
10. At the record for Brenda Lazzuri (client number 3156), insert check marks in the *UninsMotorist* field and *Collision* field for both vehicles.
11. Click in any field name and then collapse all records.
12. Remove the connection between the Clients and Coverage tables.
13. Save, print, and then close the Clients table. (Make sure the table displays in landscape orientation.)
14. Open the Coverage table, print the table, and then close the table.
15. Close **2-CopperState.accdb**.

Visual Benchmark

Create a Bookings Table

Data Files

1. Open **2-CarefreeTravel.accdb** and then create the Bookings table shown in Figure WB-2.3. You determine the data types and field sizes. Create a more descriptive caption for each field name and create a description for each field.
2. Save, print, and then close the Bookings table.
3. Create a relationship between the Agents table and Bookings table. You determine what table contains the "one" and what table contains the "many." Enforce referential integrity and cascade fields and records.
4. Create a relationship between the Tours table and Bookings table. You determine what table contains the "one" and what table contains the "many." Enforce referential integrity and cascade fields and records.
5. Save and then print the relationship report and then close the Relationships window.
6. Open the Agents table.
7. Change the *AgentID* field for Wayne Postovic from *137* to *115*.
8. Change Jenna Williamson's last name from *Williamson* to *Parr*.
9. Print and then close the Agents table.
10. Open the Bookings table, print the table, and then close the table. (Notice that the *137 AgentID* field in the Bookings table is changed to *115*. This is because the tables are related and the changes you make in the primary table are made automatically in the related table.)
11. Close **2-CarefreeTravel.accdb**.

Figure WB-2.3 Visual Benchmark Bookings Table

Booking Number ▾	Booking Date ▾	Tour ID ▾	Agent ID ▾	Number of People ▾	Click to Add ▾
1	6/1/2018	AF02	114	8	
2	6/1/2018	HC01	109	2	
3	6/3/2018	CR02	103	2	
4	6/4/2018	AK01	137	4	
5	6/5/2018	HC01	109	2	
6	6/6/2018	AT02	109	4	
7	6/8/2018	HS02	104	2	
8	6/10/2018	HC01	125	2	
9	6/11/2018	AK01	142	4	
10	6/13/2018	AT01	112	2	
11	6/15/2018	HC03	129	2	
* (New)				0	

Case Study

Part 1

You are the manager for Gold Star Cleaning Services and your company is switching over to Access for managing company data. The database designer has provided you with the database diagram in Figure WB-2.4. He wants you to follow the diagram when creating the database.

Create a new database named **2-GoldStar.accdb** and then create the Clients table shown in the database diagram. The database designer has asked you to include an appropriate caption and description for each field. Specify a field size of 3 characters for the *ClientID* field, 4 characters for the *ServiceID* field, and 1 character for the *RateID* field. You determine the field sizes for the *State*, *ZIP*, and *Telephone* fields. The designer also wants you to set the default value for the *City* field to *St. Louis* and the *State* field to *MO*. Type the following records in the table:

ClientID	101	*ClientID*	102
CoName	Smithson Realty	*CoName*	Air-Flow Systems
Address	492 Papin Street	*Address*	1058 Pine Street
City	(default value)	*City*	(default value)
State	(default value)	*State*	(default value)
ZIP	63108	*ZIP*	63186
Contact	Danielle Snowden	*Contact*	Nick Cline
Telephone	(314) 555-3588	*Telephone*	(314) 555-9452
ServiceID	GS-1	*ServiceID*	GS-3
RateID	B	*RateID*	A

ClientID	107	*ClientID*	110
CoName	Mainstreet Mortgage	*CoName*	Firstline Finances
Address	North 22nd Street	*Address*	104 Scott Avenue
City	(default value)	*City*	(default value)
State	(default value)	*State*	(default value)
ZIP	63134	*ZIP*	63126
Contact	Ted Farrell	*Contact*	Robert Styer
Telephone	(314) 555-7744	*Telephone*	(314) 555-8343
ServiceID	GS-1	*ServiceID*	GS-2
RateID	D	*RateID*	A

ClientID	112	*ClientID*	115
CoName	GB Construction	*CoName*	Simko Equipment
Address	988 Lucas Avenue	*Address*	1200 Market Street
City	(default value)	*City*	(default value)
State	(default value)	*State*	(default value)
ZIP	63175	*ZIP*	63140
Contact	Joy Ewing	*Contact*	Dale Aldrich
Telephone	(314) 555-0036	*Telephone*	(314) 555-3315
ServiceID	GS-1	*ServiceID*	GS-3
RateID	C	*RateID*	C

Figure WB-2.4 Gold Star Cleaning Services Database Diagram

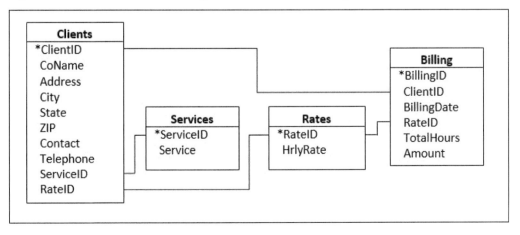

Create the Services table shown in the database diagram in Figure WB-2.4. Change the *ServiceID* field size to 4 characters. Type the following records in the table:

ServiceID	GS-1
Service	Deep cleaning all rooms and surfaces, garbage removal, recycling, carpet cleaning, disinfecting
ServiceID	GS-2
Service	Deep cleaning all rooms and surfaces, garbage removal, disinfecting
ServiceID	GS-3
Service	Deep cleaning all rooms and surfaces, disinfecting

Create the Rates table shown in the database diagram. Change the *RateID* field size to 1 character. Type the following records in the table:

RateID	A		*RateID*	B
HrlyRate	$75.50		*HrlyRate*	$65.00
RateID	C		*RateID*	D
HrlyRate	$59.75		*HrlyRate*	$50.50

Create the Billing table shown in the database diagram. Change the *BillingID* field size to 2 characters, the *ClientID* field size to 3 characters, and the *RateID* field size to 1 character. Apply the appropriate data types to the fields. Type the following records in the table:

BillingID	40		*BillingID*	41		*BillingID*	42
ClientID	101		*ClientID*	102		*ClientID*	107
BillingDate	4/1/2018		*BillingDate*	4/1/2018		*BillingDate*	4/1/2018
RateID	B		*RateID*	A		*RateID*	D
TotalHours	26		*TotalHours*	32		*TotalHours*	15
Amount	$1,690.00		*Amount*	$2,416.00		*Amount*	$747.50
BillingID	43		*BillingID*	44		*BillingID*	45
ClientID	110		*ClientID*	112		*ClientID*	115
BillingDate	4/1/2018		*BillingDate*	4/1/2018		*BillingDate*	4/1/2018
RateID	A		*RateID*	C		*RateID*	C
TotalHours	30		*TotalHours*	20		*TotalHours*	22
Amount	$2,265.00		*Amount*	$1,195.00		*Amount*	$1,314.50

Automatically adjust the column widths of each table to accommodate the longest entry and then print each table on one page. ***Hint: Check the table in Print Preview and, if necessary, change to landscape orientation and change the margins.***

Part 2

With **2-GoldStar.accdb** open, create the one-to-many relationships required to connect the tables. (Refer to Figure WB-2.4 as a guide.) You will need to increase the size of the Clients table field list box to view all of the fields. To do this, position the mouse pointer on the bottom border of the Clients table field list box in the Relationships window until the pointer turns into a white arrow pointing up and down. Press and hold down the left mouse button, drag down to the desired position, and then release the mouse button. Print the relationship report.

Part

3

Open the Services table and then make the following changes to the field values in the *ServiceID* field:

Change *GS-1* to *GS-A*
Change *GS-2* to *GS-B*
Change *GS-3* to *GS-C*

Print and then close the Services table. Open the Clients table, delete the record for client number 112, and then insert the following record:

ClientID	108
Name	Cedar Ridge Products
Address	6400 Olive Street
City	(default value)
State	(default value)
ZIP	63114
Contact	Penny Childers
Telephone	(314) 555-7660
ServiceID	GS-B
RateID	B

Print and then close the Clients table. Open the Billing table, print the table, and then close the table. Close **2-GoldStar.accdb**.

Performing Queries

> **Study Tools**

Study tools include a presentation and a list of chapter Quick Steps and Hint margin notes. Use these resources to help you further develop and review skills learned in this chapter.

> **Concepts Check**

Check your understanding by identifying application tools used in this chapter. If you are a SNAP user, launch the Concepts Check from your Assignments page.

> **Recheck**

Check your understanding by taking this quiz. If you are a SNAP user, launch the Recheck from your Assignments page.

Skills Exercise

Additional activities are available to SNAP users. If you are a SNAP user, access these activities from your Assignments page.

Skills Assessment

Assessment

1

> **Data Files**

Design Queries in a Legal Services Database

1. Open **3-WarrenLegal.accdb** and enable the content.
2. Design a query that extracts information from the Billing table with the following specifications:
   a. Include the fields *BillingID*, *ClientID*, and *CategoryID* in the query.
   b. Extract those records with the *SE* category. (Type "SE" in the field in the *Criteria* row in the *CategoryID* field column. You need to type the quotation marks to tell Access that *SE* is a criterion and not a built-in Access function.)
   c. Save the query and name it *SECategoryBillingQuery*.
   d. Print and then close the query.
3. Design a query that extracts information from the Billing table with the following specifications:
   a. Include the fields *BillingID*, *ClientID*, and *Date*.
   b. Extract those records in the *Date* field with dates between 6/8/2018 and 6/15/2018.
   c. Save the query and name it *June8-15BillingQuery*.
   d. Print and then close the query.
4. Design a query that extracts information from the Clients table with the following specifications:
   a. Include the fields *FirstName*, *LastName*, and *City*.
   b. Extract those records with cities other than Kent in the *City* field.
   c. Save the query and name it *ClientsNotInKentQuery*.
   d. Print and then close the query.

5. Design a query that extracts information from two tables with the following specifications:
   a. Include the fields *BillingID, ClientID, Date,* and *RateID* from the Billing table.
   b. Include the field *Rate* from the Rates table.
   c. Extract those records with rate IDs greater than *2*.
   d. Save the query and name it *RateIDGreaterThan2Query*.
   e. Print and then close the query.
6. Design a query that extracts information from three tables with the following specifications:
   a. Include the fields *AttorneyID, FName,* and *LName* from the Attorneys table.
   b. Include the fields *FirstName* and *LastName* from the Clients table.
   c. Include the fields *Date* and *Hours* from the Billing table.
   d. Extract those records with an attorney ID of *12*.
   e. Save the query and name it *Attorney12Query*.
   f. Print and then close the query.
7. Design a query that extracts information from four tables with the following specifications:
   a. Include the fields *AttorneyID, FName,* and *LName* from the Attorneys table.
   b. Include the field *Category* from the Categories table.
   c. Include the fields *RateID* and *Rate* from the Rates table.
   d. Include the fields *Date* and *Hours* from the Billing table.
   e. Extract those records with an attorney ID of *17* and a rate ID of 4.
   f. Save the query and name it *Attorney17RateID4Query*.
   g. Print the query in landscape orientation and then close the query.
8. Open the Attorney17RateID4Query query, click the View button on the Home tab to display the query in Design view, and then modify the query so it displays records with a rate ID of *4* and attorney IDs of *17* and *19* by making the following changes:
   a. Click below the field value "*17*" in the *AttorneyID* field column and then type 19.
   b. Click below the field value "*4*" in the *RateID* field column, type 4, and then press the Enter key.
   c. Run the query.
   d. Save the query with the new name *Attorney17&19RateID4Query*. **Hint: Do this at the Save As dialog box. Display this dialog box by clicking the File tab, clicking the Save As option, clicking the Save Object As option, and then clicking the Save As button.**
   e. Print the query in landscape orientation and then close the query.

Assessment
2

Use the Simple Query Wizard and Design Queries

1. With **3-WarrenLegal.accdb** open, use the Simple Query Wizard to extract specific information from three tables with the following specifications:
   a. At the first Simple Query Wizard dialog box, include the following fields:

   > From Attorneys table: *AttorneyID, FName,* and *LName*
   > From Categories table: *Category*
   > From Billing table: *Hours*

   b. At the second Simple Query Wizard dialog box, click the Next button.
   c. At the third Simple Query Wizard dialog box, click the *Modify the query design* option and then click the Finish button.

d. At the query window, insert *14* in the *AttorneyID* field in the *Criteria* row.
e. Run the query.
f. Save the query with the default name.
g. Print and then close the query.
2. Create a query in Design view with the Billing table with the following specifications:
a. Insert the *Hours* field from the Billing table field list box in the first, second, third, and fourth fields in the *Field* row.
b. Click the Totals button in the Show/Hide group.
c. Insert *Sum* in the first field in the *Total* row.
d. Insert *Min* in the second field in the *Total* row.
e. Insert *Max* in the third field in the *Total* row.
f. Insert *Count* in the fourth field in the *Total* row.
g. Run the query.
h. Automatically adjust the widths of the columns.
i. Save the query and name it *HoursAmountQuery*.
j. Print and then close the query.
3. Create a query in Design view with the following specifications:
a. Add the Attorneys table and Billing table to the query window.
b. Insert the *FName* field from the Attorneys table field list box in the first field in the *Field* row.
c. Insert the *LName* field from the Attorneys table field list box in the second field in the *Field* row.
d. Insert the *AttorneyID* field from the Billing table field list box in the third field in the *Field* row. (You will need to scroll down the Billing table field list box to display the *AttorneyID*.)
e. Insert the *Hours* field from the Billing table field list box in the fourth field in the *Field* row.
f. Click the Totals button in the Show/Hide group.
g. Insert *Sum* in the *Hours* field in the *Total* row.
h. Run the query.
i. Save the query and name it *AttorneyHoursQuery*.
j. Print and then close the query.
4. Create a query in Design view with the following specifications:
a. Add the Attorneys, Clients, Categories, and Billing tables to the query window.
b. Insert the *AttorneyID* field from the Attorneys table field list box in the first field in the *Field* row.
c. Insert the *ClientID* field from the Clients table field list box in the second field in the *Field* row.
d. Insert the *Category* field from the Categories table field list box in the third field in the *Field* row.
e. Insert the *Hours* field from the Billing table field list box in the fourth field in the *Field* row.
f. Run the query.
g. Save the query and name it *AttorneyClientHours*.
h. Print and then close the query.

Create a Crosstab Query and Use the Find Duplicates and Find Unmatched Query Wizards

1. With **3-WarrenLegal.accdb** open, create a crosstab query that summarizes the hours by attorney by category with the following specifications:
   a. At the first Crosstab Query Wizard dialog box, click the *Queries* option in the *View* section and then click *Query: AttorneyClientHours* in the list box.
   b. At the second Crosstab Query Wizard dialog box with *AttorneyID* selected in the *Available Fields* list box, click the One Field button.
   c. At the third Crosstab Query Wizard dialog box, click *Category* in the list box.
   d. At the fourth Crosstab Query Wizard dialog box, click *Hours* in the *Fields* list box and click *Sum* in the *Functions* list box.
   e. At the fifth Crosstab Query Wizard dialog box, select the current name in the *What do you want to name your query?* text box and then type HoursByAttorneyByCategory.
   f. Display the query in Print Preview, change to landscape orientation, change the left and right margins to 0.5 inch, and then print the query.
   g. Close the query.
2. Use the Find Duplicates Query Wizard to find those clients with the same last name with the following specifications:
   a. At the first wizard dialog box, click *Table: Clients* in the list box.
   b. At the second wizard dialog box, click *LastName* in the *Available fields* list box and then click the One Field button.
   c. At the third wizard dialog box, click the All Fields button.
   d. At the fourth wizard dialog box, name the query *DuplicateLastNamesQuery*.
   e. Print the query in landscape orientation and then close the query.
3. Use the Find Unmatched Query Wizard to find all clients who do not have any billing hours with the following specifications:
   a. At the first wizard dialog box, click *Table: Clients* in the list box.
   b. At the second wizard dialog box, click *Table: Billing* in the list box.
   c. At the third wizard dialog box, make sure *ClientID* is selected in both the *Fields in 'Clients'* list box and in the *Fields in 'Billing'* list box.
   d. At the fourth wizard dialog box, click the All Fields button to move all fields from the *Available fields* list box to the *Selected fields* list box.
   e. At the fifth wizard dialog box, click the Finish button. (Let the wizard determine the query name: *Clients Without Matching Billing*.)
   f. Print the query in landscape orientation and then close the query.

Design and Hide Fields in a Query

1. With **3-WarrenLegal.accdb** open, design the following query:
   a. At the Show Table dialog box, add the Clients table, the Billing table, and the Rates table.
   b. At the query window, insert the following fields in the *Field* row:

From the Clients table:	*FirstName, LastName*
From the Billing table:	*Hours*
From the Rates table:	*Rate*

      c. Insert in the fifth field in the *Field* row the calculated field
         Total:[Hours]*[Rate].
      d. Apply the Currency format to the *Total* column.
      e. Hide the *Hours* and *Rate* fields.
      f. Run the query.
      g. Save the query and name it *ClientBillingQuery*.
      h. Print and then close the query. (The query will print on two pages.)
  2. Close **3-WarrenLegal.accdb**.

Visual Benchmark

Create Relationships and Design a Query

1. Open **3-MRInvestments.accdb** and enable the content.
2. Display the Relationships window and then create the relationships shown
   in Figure WB-3.1. Enforce referential integrity and cascade fields and records.
   (The tables in Figure WB-3.1 have been rearranged in the Relationships
   window so you have a better view of the relationships.)
3. Save and then print the relationships.
4. Close the relationship report without saving it and then close the
   Relationships window.
5. Design the query shown in Figure WB-3.2.
6. Run the query.
7. Save the query with an appropriate name and then print the query.
8. Close **3-MRInvestments.accdb**.

Figure WB-3.1 Visual Benchmark Relationships Window

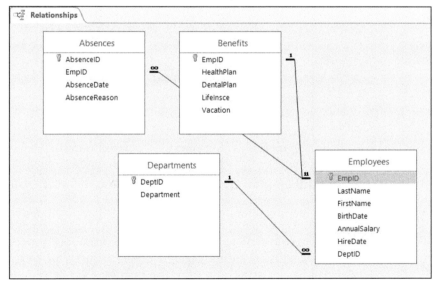

Figure WB-3.2 Visual Benchmark Query

Field:	FirstName	LastName	AnnualSalary	DeptID	Department
Table:	Employees	Employees	Employees	Departments	Departments
Sort:					
Show:	☑	☑	☑	☑	☑
Criteria:			>50000	"PR"	
or:			>50000	"RD"	

Case Study

Part

1

Data Files

You work for the Skyline Restaurant in Fort Myers, Florida. Your supervisor is reviewing the restaurant's operations and has asked for a number of query reports. Open **3-Skyline.accdb** and enable the content. Before running the queries, you realize that the tables in the restaurant database are not related. Create the following relationships (enforce referential integrity and cascade fields and records):

Field Name	"One" Table	"Many" Table
EmployeeID	Employees	Banquets
ItemID	Inventory	Orders
SupplierID	Suppliers	Orders
SupplierID	Suppliers	Inventory
EventID	Events	Banquets

Save and then print the relationships. Close the relationship report without saving it and then close the Relationships window.

Part

2

As part of the review of the restaurant's records, your supervisor has asked you for the following information. Create a separate query for each bulleted item listed below and save, name, and print the queries. (You determine the query names.)

- Suppliers in Fort Myers: From the Suppliers table, include the supplier identification number, supplier name, city, and telephone number.
- Suppliers not located in Fort Myers: From the Suppliers table, include the supplier identification number and supplier name, city, and telephone number.
- Employees hired in 2015: From the Employees table, include the employee identification number, first and last names, and hire date.

- Employees signed up for health insurance: From the Employees table, include employee first and last names and the health insurance field.
- Wedding receptions (event identification "WR") booked in the banquet room: From the Banquets table, include the reservation identification number; reservation date; event identification; and first name, last name, and telephone number of the person making the reservation.
- Banquet reservations between 6/14/2018 and 6/30/2018 and the employees making the reservations: From the Banquets table, include the reservation identification number; reservation date; and first name, last name, and telephone number of the person making the reservation; from the Employees table include the employee first and last names.
- Banquet reservations that have not been confirmed and the employees making the reservations: From the Banquets table, include the reservation identification number; reservation date; confirmed field; and first and last names of person making the reservation; from the Employees table, include employee first and last names.
- Banquet room reserved by someone whose last name begins with the letters *Wie:* From the Employees table, include the first and last names of the employee who booked the reservation; from the Banquets table, include the first and last names and telephone number of the person making the reservation.
- A query that inserts a calculated field that multiplies the number of units ordered by the unit price for all orders for supplier number *2:* From the Orders table, include the order identification number, the supplier identification number, the units ordered, and the unit price; from the Inventory table, include the item field.

Part 3

Use the Find Duplicates Query Wizard to find duplicate items in the Orders table with the following specifications:

- At the first wizard dialog box, specify the Orders table.
- At the second wizard dialog box, specify *ItemID* as the duplicate value field.
- At the third wizard dialog, specify that you want all of the fields in the query.
- At the fourth wizard dialog box, determine the query name.
- Print and then close the query.

Use the Find Unmatched Query Wizard to find all of the employees who have not made banquet reservations with the following specifications:

- At the first wizard dialog box, specify the Employees table.
- At the second wizard dialog box, specify the Banquets table.
- At the third wizard dialog box, specify the *EmployeeID* field in both list boxes.
- At the fourth wizard dialog box, specify that you want all of the fields in the query.
- At the fifth wizard dialog box, determine the query name.
- Print the query in landscape orientation with 0.5-inch left and right margins and then close the query.

Use the Crosstab Query Wizard to create a query that summarizes order amounts by supplier with the following specifications:

- At the first wizard dialog box, specify the Orders table.
- At the second wizard dialog box, specify the *SupplierID* field for row headings.

- At the third wizard dialog box, specify the *ItemID* field for column headings.
- At the fourth wizard dialog box, click *UnitPrice* in the *Fields* list box and click *Sum* in the *Functions* list box.
- At the fifth wizard dialog box, determine the query name.
- Automatically adjust the columns in the query. (You will need to scroll to the right to view and adjust all of the columns containing data.)
- Print the query in landscape orientation with 0.5-inch left and right margins and then close the query.

Part
4

Design three additional queries that require fields from at least two tables. Run the queries and then save and print the queries. In Microsoft Word, write the query information (including specific information about each query) and format the document to enhance the appearance. Save the document and name it **3-Queries**. Print and then close **3-Queries.docx**. Close **3-Skyline.accdb**.

Creating and Modifying Tables in Design View

4

> **Study Tools**

Study tools include a presentation and a list of chapter Quick Steps and Hint margin notes. Use these resources to help you further develop and review skills learned in this chapter.

> **Concepts Check**

Check your understanding by identifying application tools used in this chapter. If you are a SNAP user, launch the Concepts Check from your Assignments page.

> **Recheck**

Check your understanding by taking this quiz. If you are a SNAP user, launch the Recheck from your Assignments page.

Skills Exercise

SNAP Additional activities are available to SNAP users. If you are a SNAP user, access these activities from your Assignments page.

Skills Assessment

Assessment

1

Create an Employees Table with the Input Mask and Lookup Wizards

1. Create a new database and name it 4-Hudson.
2. Create the Employees table in Design view as shown in Figure WB-4.1 with the following specifications:
   a. Limit the *EmpID* field size to 4 characters, the *FirstName* and *LastName* fields to 20 characters, and the *Address* field to 30 characters.
   b. Create a default value of *Pueblo* for the *City* field since most of the employees live in Pueblo.
   c. Create a default value of *CO* for the *State* field, since all of the employees live in Colorado.

Figure WB-4.1 Employees Table in Design View

Field Name	Data Type	Description
EmpID	Short Text	Enter four-digit employee identification number
FirstName	Short Text	Enter employee first name
LastName	Short Text	Enter employee last name
Address	Short Text	Enter employee street address
City	Short Text	Pueblo automatically inserted
State	Short Text	CO automatically inserted
ZIP	Short Text	Enter employee ZIP code
Telephone	Short Text	Enter employee telephone number
Status	Short Text	Click down arrow and then click employee status
HireDate	Date/Time	Enter employee hire date

Figure WB-4.2 Employees Table in Datasheet View

EmpID	FirstName	LastName	Address	City	State	ZIP	Telephone	Status	HireDate	Click
1466	Samantha	O'Connell	9105 Pike Avenue	Pueblo	CO	81011	(719) 555-7658	Full-time	8/15/2016	
1790	Edward	Sorrell	9958 Franklin Avenue	Pueblo	CO	81006	(719) 555-3724	Full-time	11/15/2012	
1947	Brandon	Byrne	102 Hudson Avenue	Pueblo	CO	81012	(719) 555-1202	Full-time	8/1/2014	
1955	Leland	Hughes	4883 Caledonia Road	Pueblo	CO	81005	(719) 555-1211	Full-time	3/1/2016	
1994	Rosa	Martinez	310 Graham Avenue	Pueblo	CO	81004	(719) 555-8394	Part-time	8/15/2013	
2019	Jean	Perrault	123 Chinook Lake	Pueblo	CO	81012	(719) 555-4027	Full-time	11/15/2012	
2120	Michael	Turek	5503 East 27th Street	Boone	CO	81025	(719) 555-5423	Full-time	3/15/2014	
2301	Gregory	Nitsche	12055 East 18th Street	Pueblo	CO	81007	(719) 555-6657	Part-time	3/15/2013	
2440	Bethany	Rosario	858 West 27th Street	Pueblo	CO	81012	(719) 555-9481	Part-time	2/15/2017	
3035	Alia	Shandra	7740 West Second Street	Avondale	CO	81022	(719) 555-0059	Temporary	2/1/2016	
3129	Gloria	Cushman	6590 East 14th Street	Pueblo	CO	81006	(719) 555-0332	Temporary	5/1/2018	
3239	Rudolph	Powell	8874 Hood Avenue	Pueblo	CO	81008	(719) 555-2223	Temporary	4/1/2018	
4002	Alice	Murray	4300 East 14th Street	Pueblo	CO	81003	(719) 555-4230	Contract	9/12/2012	
4884	Simon	Banister	1022 Division Avenue	Boone	CO	81025	(719) 555-2378	Contract	5/15/2018	
*				Pueblo	CO					

    d. Create an input mask for the telephone number.

    e. Use the Lookup Wizard to specify field choices for the *Status* field and include the following choices: *Full-time*, *Part-time*, *Temporary*, and *Contract*.

3. Save the table, switch to Datasheet view, and then enter the records as shown in Figure WB-4.2.

4. Adjust the column widths.

5. Save the table and then print it in landscape orientation.

6. Switch to Design view and then add a row immediately above the *FirstName* row. Type Title in the *Field Name* field, limit the field size to 20 characters, and type the description Enter employee job title.

7. Delete the *HireDate* field.

8. Move the *Status* field so it is positioned between the *EmpID* and the *Title* rows.

9. Save the table and then switch to Datasheet view.

10. Enter the following information in the *Title* field:

EmpID	Title	EmpID	Title
1466	Design Director	2301	Assistant
1790	Assistant	2440	Assistant
1947	Resources Director	3035	Clerk
1955	Accountant	3129	Clerk
1994	Assistant	3239	Assistant
2019	Production Director	4002	Contractor
2120	Assistant	4884	Contractor

11. Apply the following text formatting to the table:

    a. Change the font to Arial and the font size to 10 points.

    b. Center the data in the *EmpID* column and the *State* column.

    c. Apply the Aqua Blue 2 alternating row color (ninth column, third row in the *Standard Colors* section).

12. Adjust the column widths.

13. Save the table and then print it in landscape orientation with left and right margins of 0.5 inch.

14. Find all occurrences of *Director* and replace them with *Manager*. **Hint: Position the insertion point in the first entry in the** Title **column and then display the Find and Replace dialog box. At the dialog box, change the** Match **option to Any Part of Field.**

15. Find all occurrences of *Assistant* and replace them with *Associate*.
16. Save the table and print it in landscape orientation with left and right margins of 0.5 inch, and then close it.
17. Sort the table by the *LastName* field in ascending order.
18. Close the table.

Assessment 2

Create a Projects Table

1. With **4-Hudson.accdb** open, create a Projects table in Design view. Include the following fields (making sure the *ProjID* field is identified as the primary key field) and create an appropriate description for each field:

Field Name	Data Type
ProjID	Short Text (field size = 4 characters)
EmpID	Short Text (field size = 4 characters)
BegDate	Date/Time
EndDate	Date/Time
EstCosts	Currency

2. Save the table, switch to Datasheet view, and then type the following data in the specified fields:

ProjID	08-A		ProjID	08-B
EmpID	2019		EmpID	1466
BegDate	8/1/2018		BegDate	8/15/2018
EndDate	10/31/2018		EndDate	12/15/2018
EstCosts	$5,250.00		EstCosts	$2,000.00
ProjID	10-A		ProjID	10-B
EmpID	1947		EmpID	2019
BegDate	10/1/2018		BegDate	10/1/2018
EndDate	1/15/2019		EndDate	12/15/2018
EstCosts	$10,000.00		EstCosts	$3,500.00
ProjID	11-A		ProjID	11-B
EmpID	1466		EmpID	1947
BegDate	11/1/2018		BegDate	11/1/2018
EndDate	2/1/2019		EndDate	3/31/2019
EstCosts	$8,000.00		EstCosts	$12,000.00

3. Adjust the column widths.
4. Save, print, and then close the Projects table.

Assessment 3

Create an Expenses Table with a Validation Rule and Input Mask

1. With **4-Hudson.accdb** open, create an Expenses table in Design view. Include the following fields (making sure the *ItemID* field is identified as the primary key field) and include an appropriate description for each field:

Field Name	Data Type
ItemID	AutoNumber
EmpID	Short Text (field size = 4 characters)
ProjID	Short Text (field size = 4 characters)
Amount	Currency (Type a condition in the *Validation Rule* property box that states the entry must be $500 or less. Type an appropriate error message in the *Validation Text* property box.)
DateSubmitted	Date/Time (Use the Input Mask to control the date so it is entered as a short date.)

2. Save the table, switch to Datasheet view, and then type the following data in the fields (recall that Access automatically fills in the *ItemID* field):

EmpID	1466	*EmpID*	2019
ProjID	08-B	*ProjID*	08-A
Amount	$245.79	*Amount*	$500.00
DateSubmitted	09/04/2018	*DateSubmitted*	09/10/2018
EmpID	4002	*EmpID*	1947
ProjID	08-B	*ProjID*	10-A
Amount	$150.00	*Amount*	$500.00
DateSubmitted	09/18/2018	*DateSubmitted*	10/03/2018
EmpID	2019	*EmpID*	1947
ProjID	10-B	*ProjID*	10-A
Amount	$487.25	*Amount*	$85.75
DateSubmitted	10/22/2018	*DateSubmitted*	10/24/2018
EmpID	1466	*EmpID*	1790
ProjID	08-B	*ProjID*	08-A
Amount	$175.00	*Amount*	$110.50
DateSubmitted	10/29/2018	*DateSubmitted*	10/30/2018
EmpID	2120	*EmpID*	1466
ProjID	10-A	*ProjID*	08-B
Amount	$75.00	*Amount*	$300.00
DateSubmitted	11/05/2018	*DateSubmitted*	11/07/2018
EmpID	1466	*EmpID*	2019
ProjID	11-A	*ProjID*	10-B
Amount	$75.00	*Amount*	$300.00
DateSubmitted	11/14/2018	*DateSubmitted*	11/19/2018

3. Adjust the column widths.
4. Insert a *Total* row with the following specifications:
   a. Click the Totals button in the Records group on the Home tab.
   b. Click in the empty field in the *Amount* column in the *Total* row.
   c. Click the down arrow at the left side of the field and then click *Sum* at the drop-down list.
   d. Click in any other field.
5. Save, print, and then close the Expenses table.
6. Create a one-to-many relationship where *EmpID* in the Employees table field list box is the "one" and *EmpID* in the Expenses table field list box is the "many." (Enforce referential integrity and cascade fields and records.)
7. Create a one-to-many relationship where *EmpID* in the Employees table field list box is the "one" and *EmpID* in the Projects table field list box is the "many." (Enforce referential integrity and cascade fields and records.)
8. Create a one-to-many relationship where *ProjID* in the Projects table field list box is the "one" and *ProjID* in the Expenses table field list box is the "many." (Enforce referential integrity and cascade fields and records.)
9. Save the relationships, print the relationship report, close the relationship report without saving it, and then close the Relationships window.

10. Design and run a query that displays all full-time employees with the following specifications:
    a. Insert the Employees table in the query window.
    b. Insert the *EmpID*, *FirstName*, *LastName*, and *Status* fields.
    c. Click the check box in the *EmpID* field in the *Show* row to remove the check mark. (This hides the EmpID numbers in the query results.)
    d. Extract full-time employees.
    e. Save the query and name it *FTEmpsQuery*.
    f. Run the query.
    g. Print and then close the query.
11. Design and run a query that displays projects managed by employee number 1947 with the following specifications:
    a. Insert the Employees table and Projects table in the query window.
    b. Insert the *EmpID*, *FirstName*, and *LastName* fields from the Employees table field list box.
    c. Insert the *ProjID* field from the Projects table field list box.
    d. Extract those projects managed by employee number 1947.
    e. Save the query and name it *ProjsByEmp1947Query*.
    f. Run the query.
    g. Print and then close the query.
12. Design and run a query that displays expense amounts over $250 and the employees submitting the expenses with the following specifications:
    a. Insert the Expenses table and Employees table in the query window.
    b. Insert the *ItemID*, *Amount*, and *DateSubmitted* fields from the Expenses table field list box.
    c. Insert the *FirstName* and *LastName* fields from the Employees table field list box.
    d. Hide the *ItemID* field in the query results by clicking the check box in the *ItemID* field in the *Show* row to remove the check mark.
    e. Extract those expense amounts over $250.
    f. Save the query and name it *ExpensesOver$250Query*.
    g. Run the query.
    h. Print and then close the query.
13. Design and run a query that displays expenses submitted by employee number 1947 with the following specifications:
    a. Insert the Employees table and Expenses table in the query window.
    b. Insert the *EmpID*, *FirstName*, and *LastName* fields from the Employees table field list box.
    c. Insert the *ProjID*, *Amount*, and *DateSubmitted* from the Expenses table field list box.
    d. Click the check box in the *EmpID* field in the *Show* row to remove the check mark. (This hides the EmpID numbers in the query results.)
    e. Extract those expenses submitted by employee number 1947.
    f. Save the query and name it *ExpensesBy1947Query*.
    g. Run the query.
    h. Print and then close the query.

Edit the Employees Table

1. With **4-Hudson.accdb** open, open the Employees table.
2. Display the table in Design view, click in the *ZIP* field in the *Data Type* column, and then click in the *Input Mask* property box in the *Field Properties* section.
3. Use the Input Mask Wizard to create a nine-digit zip code input mask.
4. Save the table and then switch to Datasheet view.
5. Delete the records for employee number 3035 (Alia Shandra), employee number 3129 (Gloria Cushman), and employee number 4884 (Simon Banister).
6. Insert the following new records:

EmpID	2286	*EmpID*	2970
Status	Full-time	*Status*	Full-time
Title	Associate	*Title*	Associate
FirstName	Erica	*FirstName*	Daniel
LastName	Bonari	*LastName*	Ortiz
Address	4850 55th Street	*Address*	12021 Cedar Lane
City	(Pueblo automatically inserted)	*City*	(Pueblo automatically inserted)
State	(CO automatically inserted)	*State*	(CO automatically inserted)
ZIP	81005-5002	*ZIP*	81011-1255
Telephone	(719) 555-1293	*Telephone*	(719) 555-0790

7. Adjust the width of the *ZIP* column. (Only the two new records will contain the nine-digit zip code.)
8. Save the Employees table.
9. Display the table in Print Preview, change to landscape orientation, and then change the left and right margins to 0.5 inch. Print and then close the table.
10. Close **4-Hudson.accdb**.

Visual Benchmark

Data Files

Design and Format a Query

1. Open **4-AlpineServices.accdb** and enable the content.
2. Design and run the query shown in Figure WB-4.3. (Make sure you include the calculated field to determine the order totals and the *Total* row.)
3. Change the font for the data in the query to 12-point Candara, add an alternating row color, and adjust column widths so your query displays in a manner similar to the query in Figure WB-4.3.
4. Save, print the query in landscape orientation, and then close the query.
5. Close **4-AlpineServices.accdb**.

Figure WB-4.3 Visual Benchmark

OrderDate ▾	SupplierName ▾	ProductID ▾	UnitsOrdered ▾	UnitPrice ▾	Total ▾
5/4/2018	Manning, Inc.	101-S2R	15	$129.95	1949.25
5/4/2018	Manning, Inc.	101-S3B	15	$119.95	1799.25
5/4/2018	Freedom Corporation	209-L	25	$6.95	173.75
5/4/2018	Freedom Corporation	209-XL	25	$7.20	180
5/4/2018	Freedom Corporation	209-XXL	20	$7.29	145.8
5/4/2018	Freedom Corporation	210-L	25	$6.49	162.25
5/4/2018	Freedom Corporation	210-M	15	$6.49	97.35
5/18/2018	Sound Supplies	299-M2	10	$88.79	887.9
5/18/2018	Sound Supplies	299-M3	10	$88.79	887.9
5/18/2018	Sound Supplies	299-M5	10	$88.79	887.9
5/18/2018	Sound Supplies	299-W1	8	$75.29	602.32
5/18/2018	Sound Supplies	299-W3	10	$75.29	752.9
5/18/2018	Sound Supplies	299-W4	10	$75.29	752.9
5/18/2018	Sound Supplies	299-W5	10	$75.29	752.9
5/18/2018	Emerald City Products	602-XR	5	$429.00	2145
Total				**$1,280.85**	**12177.37**

Case Study

Part

1

Data Files

You work for Blue Ridge Enterprises and your supervisor has asked you to create tables with information about representatives and clients. Open **4-BlueRidge.accdb**, enable the content, and then create a Representatives table with the following fields:

- Create a field for the representative identification number, change the data type to Short Text, and limit the field size to 3 characters. (This is the primary key field.)
- Create a field for the representative's first name and limit the field size to 20 characters.
- Create a field for the representative's last name and limit the field size to 20 characters.
- Create a field for the representative's telephone number and use the Input Mask Wizard.
- Create a field for the insurance plan and use the Lookup Wizard and include four options: *Platinum*, *Premium*, *Standard*, and *None*.
- Create a field for the yearly bonus amount, type a validation rule that states the bonus must be less than $10,001, and include an error message. (You determine the message.)

In Datasheet view, enter six records in the table. (You determine the data to enter.) When entering the data, make sure that at least two representatives will receive a yearly bonus over $5,000 and that at least two representatives are signed up for the *Platinum* insurance plan. Insert a *Total* row that sums the yearly bonus amounts. Change the font for the data in the table to Cambria, change the font size to 10 points, and apply a light green alternating row color. Center the data in the representative identification column. Adjust the column widths and then save the Representatives table. Print the table in landscape orientation and then close the table.

Part 2

With **4-BlueRidge.accdb** open, create a second table named Clients (containing information on companies doing business with Blue Ridge Enterprises) with the following fields:

- Create a field for the client identification number and limit the field size to 2 characters. (This is the primary key field.)
- Create a field for the representative identification number (using the same field name you used in Part 1 in the Representatives table) and limit the field size to 3 characters.
- Create fields for the company name, address, city, state (or province), and zip (or postal code). Insert the city you live in as the default value for the city field and insert the two-letter state or province abbreviation where you live as the default value for the state or province field.
- Create a field for the client's telephone number and use the Input Mask.
- Create a field for the client's type of business and insert the word *Wholesaler* as the default value.

In Datasheet view, enter at least eight companies. (You determine the data to enter.) Make sure you use the representative identification numbers in the Clients table that match numbers in the Representatives table. Identify at least one company as a *Retailer*, rather than a *Wholesaler*, and make at least one representative represent two or more companies. Change the font for the data in the table to Cambria, change the font size to 10 points, and apply a light green alternating row color (the same color you chose in Part 1). Center the data in the client identification column, the representative identification column, and the state (or province) column. Adjust the column widths and then save the Clients table. Print the table in landscape orientation and then close the table.

Part 3

Create a one-to-many relationship with the representative identification number in the Representatives table as the "one" and the representative identification number in the Clients table as the "many." (Enforce referential integrity and cascade fields and records.) Save the relationship, print the relationship report, and then close the report without saving it.

Part 4

Your supervisor has asked you for specific information about representatives and clients. To provide answers to your supervisor, create and print the following queries:

- Create a query that extracts records of representatives earning a yearly bonus over $5,000. (You determine the fields to insert in the query window.) Save, print, and then close the query.
- Create a query that extracts records of representatives signed up for the Platinum insurance plan. (You determine the fields to insert in the query window.) Save, print, and then close the query.
- Create a query that extracts records of wholesale clients. (You determine the fields to insert in the query window.) Save, print, and then close the query.
- Create a query that extracts records of companies represented by a specific representative. (Use a representative identification number you entered in Part 2 that represents two or more companies.) Save, print, and then close the query and then close the database.

Microsoft Access® Level 1

Unit 1 Performance Assessment

Assessing Proficiency

In this unit, you have learned to design, create, and modify tables and to create one-to-many relationships and one-to-one relationships between tables. You have also learned how to perform queries on data in tables.

Assessment

1

Create Tables in a Cornerstone Catering Database

1. Use Access to create tables for Cornerstone Catering. Name the database **U1-Cornerstone**. Create a table named *Employees* that includes the following fields. If no data type is specified for a field, use the Short Text data type. You determine the field size and specify the same field size for a field that is contained in different tables. For example, if you specify a field size of 2 characters for the *EmployeeID* field in the Employees table, specify a field size of 2 characters for the *EmployeeID* field in the Events table. Provide a description for each field.

   EmployeeID (primary key field)
   FirstName
   LastName
   CellPhone (Use the Input Mask Wizard for this field.)

2. After creating the table, switch to Datasheet view and then enter the following data in the appropriate fields:

EmployeeID	10		*EmployeeID*	14
FirstName	Erin		*FirstName*	Mikio
LastName	Jergens		*LastName*	Ogami
CellPhone	(505) 555-3193		*CellPhone*	(505) 555-1087
EmployeeID	19		*EmployeeID*	21
FirstName	Martin		*FirstName*	Isabelle
LastName	Vaughn		*LastName*	Baptista
CellPhone	(505) 555-4461		*CellPhone*	(505) 555-4425
EmployeeID	24		*EmployeeID*	26
FirstName	Shawn		*FirstName*	Madison
LastName	Kettering		*LastName*	Harris
CellPhone	(505) 555-3885		*CellPhone*	(505) 555-2256

EmployeeID	28	EmployeeID	30
FirstName	Victoria	*FirstName*	Isaac
LastName	Lamesa	*LastName*	Hobart
CellPhone	(505) 555-6650	*CellPhone*	(505) 555-7430
EmployeeID	32	*EmployeeID*	35
FirstName	Lester	*FirstName*	Manuela
LastName	Franklin	*LastName*	Harte
CellPhone	(505) 555-0440	*CellPhone*	(505) 555-1221

3. Change the font for data in the table to Cambria, change the font size to 10 points, and apply a light blue alternating row color. Center-align the data in the *EmployeeID* column.
4. Adjust the column widths.
5. Save, print, and then close the Employees table.
6. Create a table named *Plans* that includes the following fields:

   PlanCode (primary key field)
   Plan

7. After creating the table, switch to Datasheet view and then enter the following data in the appropriate fields:

PlanCode	A	*PlanCode*	B
Plan	Sandwich Buffet	*Plan*	Cold Luncheon Buffet
PlanCode	C	*PlanCode*	D
Plan	Hot Luncheon Buffet	*Plan*	Combination Dinner
PlanCode	E	*PlanCode*	F
Plan	Vegetarian Luncheon Buffet	*Plan:*	Vegetarian Dinner Buffet
PlanCode	G	*PlanCode*	H
Plan	Seafood Luncheon Buffet	*Plan*	Seafood Dinner Buffet

8. Change the font for data in the table to Cambria, change the font size to 10 points, and apply the Blue, Accent 1, Lighter 80% alternating row color (fifth column, second row in the *Theme Colors* section). Center-align the data in the *PlanCode* column.
9. Adjust the column widths.
10. Save, print, and then close the Plans table.
11. Create a table named *Prices* that includes the following fields:

    PriceCode (primary key field)
    PricePerPerson (Identify as the Currency data type.)

12. After creating the table, switch to Datasheet view and then enter the following data in the appropriate fields:

PriceCode	1	*PriceCode*	2
PricePerPerson	$11.50	*PricePerPerson*	$12.75
PriceCode	3	*PriceCode*	4
PricePerPerson	$14.50	*PricePerPerson*	$16.00
PriceCode	5	*PriceCode*	6
PricePerPerson	$18.50	*PricePerPerson*	$21.95

13. Change the font for data in the table to Cambria, change the font size to 10 points, and apply the Blue, Accent 1, Lighter 80% alternating row color. Center-align the data in both columns.
14. Adjust the column widths.

15. Save, print, and then close the Prices table.
16. Create a table named *Clients* that includes the following fields:

> *ClientID* (primary key field)
> *ClientName*
> *StreetAddress*
> *City*
> *State* (Insert *NM* as the default value.)
> *ZIP*
> *Telephone* (Use the Input Mask Wizard for this field.)

17. After creating the table, switch to Datasheet view and then enter the following data in the appropriate fields:

ClientID	104	*ClientID*	155
ClientName	Sarco Corporation	*ClientName*	Creative Concepts
StreetAddress	340 Cordova Road	*StreetAddress*	1026 Market Street
City	Santa Fe	*City*	Los Alamos
State	NM	*State*	NM
ZIP	87510	*ZIP*	87547
Telephone	(505) 555-3880	*Telephone*	(505) 555-1200
ClientID	218	*ClientID*	286
ClientName	Allenmore Systems	*ClientName*	Sol Enterprises
StreetAddress	7866 Second Street	*StreetAddress*	120 Cerrillos Road
City	Espanola	*City*	Santa Fe
State	NM	*State*	NM
ZIP	87535	*ZIP*	87560
Telephone	(505) 555-3455	*Telephone*	(505) 555-7700
ClientID	295	*ClientID*	300
ClientName	Benson Productions	*ClientName*	Old Town Corporation
StreetAddress	555 Junction Road	*StreetAddress*	1035 East Adams Way
City	Santa Fe	*City*	Santa Fe
State	NM	*State*	NM
ZIP	87558	*ZIP*	87561
Telephone	(505) 555-8866	*Telephone*	(505) 555-2125
ClientID	305	*ClientID*	350
ClientName	Cromwell Company	*ClientName*	GH Manufacturing
StreetAddress	752 Rialto Way	*StreetAddress*	9550 Stone Road
City	Santa Fe	*City*	Los Alamos
State	NM	*State*	NM
ZIP	87512	*ZIP*	87547
Telephone	(505) 555-7500	*Telephone*	(505) 555-3388

18. Change the font for data in the table to Cambria, change the font size to 10 points, and apply the Blue, Accent 1, Lighter 80% alternating row color. Center-align the data in the *ClientID* column.
19. Adjust the column widths.
20. Save the table and then print it in landscape orientation.
21. Close the Clients table.

22. Create a table named *Events* that includes the following fields:

> *EventID* (primary key field) (Identify as the AutoNumber data type.)
> *ClientID*
> *EmployeeID*
> *DateOfEvent* (Identify as the Date/Time data type.)
> *PlanCode*
> *PriceCode*
> *NumberOfPeople* (Identify as the Number data type.)

23. After creating the table, switch to Datasheet view and then enter the following data in the appropriate fields:

EventID	(AutoNumber)	*EventID*	(AutoNumber)
ClientID	218	*ClientID*	104
EmployeeID	14	*EmployeeID*	19
DateOfEvent	7/11/2018	*DateOfEvent*	7/12/2018
PlanCode	B	*PlanCode*	D
PriceCode	3	*PriceCode*	5
NumberOfPeople	250	*NumberOfPeople*	120
EventID	(AutoNumber)	*EventID*	(AutoNumber)
ClientID	155	*ClientID*	286
EmployeeID	24	*EmployeeID*	10
DateOfEvent	7/17/2018	*DateOfEvent*	7/18/2018
PlanCode	A	*PlanCode*	C
PriceCode	1	*PriceCode*	4
NumberOfPeople	300	*NumberOfPeople*	75
EventID	(AutoNumber)	*EventID*	(AutoNumber)
ClientID	218	*ClientID*	104
EmployeeID	14	*EmployeeID*	10
DateOfEvent	7/19/2018	*DateOfEvent*	7/22/2018
PlanCode	C	*PlanCode*	B
PriceCode	4	*PriceCode*	3
NumberOfPeople	50	*NumberOfPeople*	30
EventID	(AutoNumber)	*EventID*	(AutoNumber)
ClientID	305	*ClientID*	295
EmployeeID	30	*EmployeeID*	35
DateOfEvent	7/24/2018	*DateOfEvent*	7/25/2018
PlanCode	H	*PlanCode*	E
PriceCode	6	*PriceCode*	4
NumberOfPeople	150	*NumberOfPeople*	75
EventID	(AutoNumber)	*EventID*	(AutoNumber)
ClientID	300	*ClientID*	350
EmployeeID	32	*EmployeeID*	28
DateOfEvent	7/26/2018	*DateOfEvent*	7/30/2018
PlanCode	B	*PlanCode*	D
PriceCode	3	*PriceCode*	6
NumberOfPeople	200	*NumberOfPeople*	100

24. Change the font for data in the table to Cambria, change the font size to 10 points, and apply the Blue, Accent 1, Lighter 80% alternating row color. Center-align the data in all of the columns except the *DateOfEvent* column.

25. Adjust the column widths.
26. Save the table and then print it in landscape orientation.
27. Close the Events table.

Assessment 2

Create Relationships between Tables

1. With **U1-Cornerstone.accdb** open, create the following one-to-many relationships, enforce referential integrity, and cascade fields and records:
   a. *ClientID* in the Clients table is the "one" and *ClientID* in the Events table is the "many."
   b. *EmployeeID* in the Employees table is the "one" and *EmployeeID* in the Events table is the "many."
   c. *PlanCode* in the Plans table is the "one" and *PlanCode* in the Events table is the "many."
   d. *PriceCode* in the Prices table is the "one" and *PriceCode* in the Events table is the "many."
2. Save and then print the relationship report in landscape orientation.
3. Close the relationship report without saving it and then close the Relationships window.

Assessment 3

Modify Tables

1. With **U1-Cornerstone.accdb** open, open the Plans table in Datasheet view and then add the following record at the end of the table:

   PlanCode I
   Plan   Hawaiian Luau Dinner Buffet

2. Adjust the column widths.
3. Save, print, and then close the Plans table.
4. Open the Events table in Datasheet view and then add the following record at the end of the table:

EventID	(AutoNumber)	PlanCode	I
ClientID	104	PriceCode	5
EmployeeID	21	NumberOfPeople	125
Date	7/31/2018		

5. Save, print (in landscape orientation), and then close the Events table.

Assessment 4

Design Queries

1. With **U1-Cornerstone.accdb** open, create a query to extract records from the Events table with the following specifications:
   a. Include the fields *ClientID*, *DateOfEvent*, and *PlanCode*.
   b. Extract those records with a PlanCode of C. (You will need to type "C" in the *Criteria* row.)
   c. Run the query.
   d. Save the query and name it *PlanCodeCQuery*.
   e. Print and then close the query.
2. Extract records from the Clients table with the following specifications:
   a. Include the fields *ClientName*, *City*, and *Telephone*.
   b. Extract those records with a city of Santa Fe.
   c. Run the query.
   d. Save the query and name it *SantaFeClientsQuery*.
   e. Print and then close the query.

3. Extract information from two tables with the following specifications:
   a. From the Clients table, include the fields *ClientName* and *Telephone*.
   b. From the Events table, include the fields *DateOfEvent*, *PlanCode*, and *NumberOfPeople*.
   c. Extract those records with dates between July 1, 2018, and July 15, 2018.
   d. Run the query.
   e. Save the query and name it *July1-15EventsQuery*.
   f. Print and then close the query.

Assessment 5

Design a Query with a Calculated Field Entry

1. With **U1-Cornerstone.accdb** open, create a query in Design view with the Events table and Prices table and insert the following fields in the specified locations:
   a. Insert *EventID* from the Events table field list box in the first field in the *Field* row.
   b. Insert *DateOfEvent* from the Events table field list box in the second field in the *Field* row.
   c. Insert *NumberOfPeople* from the Events table field list box in the third field in the *Field* row.
   d. Insert *PricePerPerson* from the Prices table field list box in the fourth field in the *Field* row.
2. Insert the following calculated field entry in the fifth field in the *Field* row: *Amount:[NumberOfPeople]*[PricePerPerson]*.
3. Run the query.
4. Save the query and name it *EventAmountsQuery*.
5. Print and then close the query.

Assessment 6

Design a Query with Aggregate Functions

1. With **U1-Cornerstone.accdb** open, create a query in Design view using the EventAmountsQuery query with the following specifications:
   a. Click the Create tab and then click the Query Design button.
   b. At the Show Tables dialog box, click the Queries tab.
   c. Double-click *EventAmountsQuery* in the list box and then click the Close button.
   d. Insert the *Amount* field in the first, second, third, and fourth fields in the *Field* row.
   e. Click the Totals button in the Show/Hide group.
   f. Insert *Sum* in the first field in the *Total* row.
   g. Insert *Avg* in the second field in the *Total* row.
   h. Insert *Min* in the third field in the *Total* row.
   i. Insert *Max* in the fourth field in the *Total* row.
2. Run the query.
3. Automatically adjust the column widths.
4. Save the query and name it *AmountTotalsQuery*.
5. Print and then close the query.

Assessment 7

Design a Query Using Fields from Tables and a Query

1. With **U1-Cornerstone.accdb** open, create a query in Design view using the Employees table, Clients table, Events table, and EventAmountsQuery query with the following specifications:
   a. Click the Create tab and then click the Query Design button.
   b. At the Show Tables dialog box, double-click *Employees*.
   c. Double-click *Clients*.
   d. Double-click *Events*.
   e. Click the Queries tab, double-click *EventAmountsQuery* in the list box, and then click the Close button.
   f. Insert the *LastName* field from the Employees table field list box in the first field in the *Field* row.
   g. Insert the *ClientName* field from the Clients table field list box in the second field in the *Field* row.
   h. Insert the *Amount* field from EventAmountsQuery table field list box in the third field in the *Field* row.
   i. Insert the *DateOfEvent* field from the Events table field list box in the fourth field in the *Field* row.
2. Run the query.
3. Save the query and name it *EmployeeEventsQuery*.
4. Close the query.
5. Using the Crosstab Query Wizard, create a query that summarizes the total event amounts by employee and by client using the following specifications:
   a. At the first Crosstab Query Wizard dialog box, click the *Queries* option in the *View* section and then click *Query: EmployeeEventsQuery* in the list box.
   b. At the second Crosstab Query Wizard dialog box, click *LastName* in the *Available Fields* list box and then click the One Field button.
   c. At the third Crosstab Query Wizard dialog box, make sure *ClientName* is selected in the list box.
   d. At the fourth Crosstab Query Wizard dialog box, make sure *Amount* is selected in the *Fields* list box and then click *Sum* in the *Functions* list box.
   e. At the fifth Crosstab Query Wizard dialog box, type AmountsByEmployeeByClientQuery in the *What do you want to name your query?* text box.
6. Automatically adjust the column widths.
7. Print the query in landscape orientation and then close the query.

Assessment 8

Use the Find Duplicates Query Wizard

1. With **U1-Cornerstone.accdb** open, use the Find Duplicates Query Wizard to find employees who are responsible for at least two events with the following specifications:
   a. At the first wizard dialog box, double-click *Table: Events* in the list box.
   b. At the second wizard dialog box, click *EmployeeID* in the *Available fields* list box and then click the One Field button.
   c. At the third wizard dialog box, move the *DateOfEvent* field and the *NumberOfPeople* field from the *Available fields* list box to the *Additional query fields* list box.
   d. At the fourth wizard dialog box, name the query *DuplicateEventsQuery*.
2. Print and then close the query.

Use the Find Unmatched Query Wizard

1. With **U1-Cornerstone.accdb** open, use the Find Unmatched Query Wizard to find employees who do not have upcoming events scheduled with the following specifications:

   a. At the first wizard dialog box, click *Table: Employees* in the list box.

   b. At the second wizard dialog box, click *Table: Events* in the list box.

   c. At the third wizard dialog box, make sure *EmployeeID* is selected in the *Fields in 'Employees'* list box and in the *Fields in 'Events'* list box.

   d. At the fourth wizard dialog box, click the All Fields button to move all fields from the *Available fields* list box to the *Selected fields* list box.

   e. At the fifth wizard dialog box, click the Finish button. (Let the wizard determine the query name: *Employees Without Matching Events*.)

2. Print and then close the *Employees Without Matching Events* query.

Writing Activities

The following activity gives you the opportunity to practice your writing skills along with demonstrating an understanding of some of the important Access features you have mastered in this unit. Use correct grammar, appropriate word choices, and clear sentence constructions.

Create a Payroll Table and Word Report

The manager of Cornerstone Catering has asked you to add information to the **U1-Cornerstone.accdb** database on employee payroll. You need to create another table that will contain information on payroll. The manager wants the table to include the following information: (You determine the appropriate field names, data types, field sizes, and descriptions.)

Employee Number	10		*Employee Number*	14
Status	Full-time		*Status*	Part-time
Monthly Salary	$2,850		*Monthly Salary*	$1,500
Employee Number	19		*Employee Number*	21
Status	Part-time		*Status*	Full-time
Monthly Salary	$1,400		*Monthly Salary*	$2,500
Employee Number	24		*Employee Number*	26
Status	Part-time		*Status*	Part-time
Monthly Salary	$1,250		*Monthly Salary*	$1,000
Employee Number	28		*Employee Number*	30
Status	Full-time		*Status*	Part-time
Monthly Salary	$2,500		*Monthly Salary*	$3,000
Employee Number	32		*Employee Number*	35
Status	Full-time		*Status*	Full-time
Monthly Salary	$2,300		*Monthly Salary*	$2,750

Print and then close the payroll table. Open Word and then write a report to the manager detailing how you created the table. Include a title for the report, steps on how the table was created, and any other pertinent information. Save the completed report and name it **U1-TableRpt**. Print and then close **U1-TableRpt.docx** and then close Word.

Internet Research

Vehicle Search

In this activity, you will search the Internet for information on different vehicles before completing actual test drives. Researching a major product, such as a vehicle, before you make your purchase can increase your chances of finding a good buy, potentially guide you away from making a poor purchase, and help speed up the process of narrowing the search to the type of vehicle that will best meet your needs. Before you begin, list the top five criteria you would look for in a vehicle. For example, it must be a four-door vehicle, needs to be four-wheel drive, and so on.

Using key search words, find at least two websites that provide vehicle reviews. Use the search engines provided within the different review sites to find vehicles that fulfill the criteria you listed. Create a database in Access and create a table in that database that will contain the results from your vehicle search. Design the table to accommodate the types of data you need to record for each vehicle that meets your requirements. Include at least the make, model, year, price, and description in the table. Also include the ability to rate the vehicle as poor, fair, good, or excellent. You will decide on the rating of each vehicle depending on your findings. Print the table you created and then close the database.

Microsoft®

Access® Level 1

Unit 2

Creating Forms and Reports

Creating Forms

Study Tools

Study tools include a presentation and a list of chapter Quick Steps and Hint margin notes. Use these resources to help you further develop and review skills learned in this chapter.

Concepts Check

Check your understanding by identifying application tools used in this chapter. If you are a SNAP user, launch the Concepts Check from your Assignments page.

Recheck

Check your understanding by taking this quiz. If you are a SNAP user, launch the Recheck from your Assignments page.

Skills Exercise

Additional activities are available to SNAP users. If you are a SNAP user, access these activities from your Assignments page.

Skills Assessment

Assessment

1

Data Files

Create and Customize a Suppliers Form

1. Open **5-PacTrek.accdb** and enable the content.
2. Use the Form button in the Forms group on the Create tab to create a form with the Suppliers table.
3. Switch to Form view and then add the following records to the Suppliers form:

SupplierID	12
SupplierName	Seaside Suppliers
StreetAddress	4120 Shoreline Drive
City	Vancouver
Prov/State	BC
PostalCode	V2V 8K4
EmailAddress	seaside@emcp.net
Telephone	6045557945

SupplierID	34
SupplierName	Carson Company
StreetAddress	120 Plaza Center
City	Vancouver
Prov/State	BC
PostalCode	V2V 1K6
EmailAddress	carson@emcp.net
Telephone	6045551955

4. Delete the record containing information on Manning, Inc.
5. Switch to Layout view and then apply the Organic theme to the form.
6. Select and delete the logo object in the *Form Header* section and then click the Logo button in the Header/Footer group. At the Insert Picture dialog box, navigate to the AL1C5 folder on your storage medium and then double-click *River.jpg*.
7. Type Pacific Trek Suppliers as the title for the form. Click in any field outside the title and then click the title (which selects the header control object). Drag the right border of the title control object to the left until the border displays near the title.
8. Insert the date and time in the *Form Header* section.
9. Select the date and time control objects, drag in the left border until the border displays near the date and time, and then drag the objects so they are positioned near the title.
10. Click the text box control object containing the supplier number and then drag the right border to the left until *Lines: 1 Characters: 30* displays at the left side of the Status bar.
11. Select the fields in the first column (*SupplierID* through *Telephone*) and then apply the following formatting:
    a. Apply bold formatting.
    b. Apply the Dark Blue font color (ninth column, bottom row in the *Standard Colors* section).
    c. Apply the Align Right alignment.
    d. Apply the Light Blue 2 shape fill (fifth column, third row in the *Standard Colors* section).
    e. Apply the Dark Blue shape outline color (ninth column, bottom row in the *Standard Colors* section).
12. Select the second column and then apply the following formatting:
    a. Apply the Light Blue 1 shape fill (fifth column, second row in the *Standard Colors* section).
    b. Apply the Dark Blue shape outline color (ninth column, bottom row in the *Standard Colors* section).
13. Switch to Form view.
14. Save the form with the name *Suppliers*.
15. Make active the record for supplier number 12 (one of the new records you entered) and then print the record. (Make sure you print only the record for supplier number 12.)
16. Make active the record for supplier number 34 and then print the record.
17. Close the Suppliers table.

Assessment 2

Create and Customize an Orders Form

1. With **5-PacTrek.accdb** open, create a form with the Orders table using the Form button on the Create tab.
2. Insert a field from a related table by completing the following steps:
    a. Display the Field List task pane and then, if necessary, click the Show all tables hyperlink.
    b. Expand the Suppliers table in the *Fields available in related tables* section.

    c. Drag the *SupplierName* field into the form and position it between *SupplierID* and *ProductID*.

    d. Change the *SupplierName* field from a Lookup field to a text box by clicking the Options button below the field and then clicking *Change to Text Box* at the drop-down list.

    e. Close the Field List task pane.

3. Click the text box control object containing the text *1010* and then drag the right border to the left until *Lines: 1 Characters: 30* displays at the left side of the Status bar.

4. Select all of the objects in the *Detail* section by clicking an object in the *Detail* section and then clicking the table move handle (the small, square button with a four-headed arrow inside). With the objects selected, apply the following formatting:

    a. Change the font to Cambria and the font size to 12 points.

    b. Apply the Align Right alignment.

5. Select the first column and then apply the following formatting:

    a. Apply the Green 2 shape fill (seventh column, third row in the *Standard Colors* section).

    b. Apply bold formatting.

6. Apply conditional formatting that changes the font color to standard blue for any *Amount* field entry that contains an amount greater than $999. ***Hint: Click the text box control object containing the amount $199.50, click the Conditional Formatting button, click the New Rule button, change the second option in the* Edit the rule description *section to greater than, and then enter 999 in the third option box (without the dollar symbol).***

7. Insert a text box control object below the *Amount* field. Type Plus 8% Tax in the new label control object. Click in the new text box control object, display the Property Sheet task pane with the Data tab selected, and then type a formula in the *Control Source* property box that multiplies the amount by 1.08. Apply currency formatting to the amounts in the new text box control object.

8. Save the form with the name *Orders*.

9. Print the fifteenth record in the form and then close the form.

Assessment 3 — Create a Split Form With the Products Table

1. With **5-PacTrek.accdb** open, create a form with the Products table using the *Split Form* option from the More Forms button drop-down list.

2. Decrease the width of the second column until *Lines: 1 Characters: 35* displays at the left side of the Status bar.

3. Select the first column and then apply the following formatting:

    a. Apply bold formatting.

    b. Apply the Aqua Blue 1 shape fill (ninth column, second row in the *Standard Colors* section).

    c. Apply the Blue shape outline color (eighth column, bottom row in the *Standard Colors* section).

4. Click in the text box control object containing the number *0* (the *UnitsOnOrder* number) and then apply conditional formatting that displays the number in red in any field value equal to zero.

5. Change to Form view, create a new record, and then enter the following information in the specified fields:

ProductID	205-CS
Product	Timberline solo cook set
SupplierID	15
UnitsInStock	8
UnitsOnOrder	0
ReorderLevel	5

6. Save the form with the name *Products*.
7. Print the form with the current record displayed (the record you just typed). ***Hint: At the Print dialog box, click the Setup button. At the Page Setup dialog box, click the Print Form Only option.***
8. Close the Products form.
9. Close **5-PacTrek.accdb**.

Visual Benchmark

Create and Format a Properties Form

1. Open **5-SunProperties.accdb** and enable the content.
2. Create a form with the Properties table and format the form so it appears similar to the form in Figure WB-5.1 using the following specifications:
   a. Apply the Facet theme and apply the Paper theme colors.
   b. Insert the logo, title, date, and time in the *Form Header* section, as shown in the figure. (Insert the file **SunPropLogo.jpg** for the logo. Adjust the size of the title control object and then move the date and time, as shown in the figure.)
   c. Select all of the objects in the *Detail* section and then change the font color to Maroon 5 (sixth column, sixth row in the *Standard Colors* section).

Figure WB-5.1 Visual Benchmark

d. Select the first column; apply bold formatting; apply Light Yellow, Background 2, Darker 10% shape fill (third column, second row in the *Theme Colors* section); apply the Maroon 5 shape outline color (sixth column, sixth row in the *Standard Colors* section); and then change the alignment to Align Right.

e. Decrease the size of the second column as shown in the figure.

f. Insert a new column to the right of the second column, merge cells in the new column to accommodate the sun image, and then insert the image **SunProp.jpg** (as a control object). Adjust the width of the third column so the image displays as shown in Figure WB-5.1.

g. Apply conditional formatting to the *MoRent* field that displays any rent amount greater than $999 in green.

h. Adjust the position of the control objects so that the form displays similarly to what is shown in Figure WB-5.1.

3. Save the form with the name *Properties* and then print the current record.

4. Close the form and then close **5-SunProperties.accdb**.

Case Study

Part 1

Data Files

You are the office manager at the Lewis Vision Care Center and your center is switching over to Access to manage files. You have already created four basic tables and now need to create relationships and enter data. Open **5-LewisCenter.accdb**, enable the content, and then create the following relationships between tables (enforce referential integrity and cascade fields and records):

Field Name	"One" Table	"Many" Table
PatientID	Patients	Billing
ServiceID	Services	Billing
DoctorID	Doctors	Billing

Save and then print the relationships.

Part 2

Before entering data in the tables, create a form for each table and apply a theme of your choosing. Enter data in the forms in the order in which it appears in Figure WB-5.2 (on the next page). Apply any additional formatting to enhance the appearance of each form. After entering the information in the forms, print the first record of each form.

Part 3

Apply the following conditions to fields in forms:

• In the Patients form, apply the condition that the city *Tulsa* displays in red and the city *Broken Arrow* displays in blue in the *City* field. Print the first record of the Patients form and then close the form.

• In the Billing form, apply the condition that amounts over $99 in the *Fee* field display in green. Print the second record of the Billing form and then close the form.

Close **C5-LewisCenter.accdb**.

Part

4

Your center has a procedures manual that describes workplace processes and procedures. Open Word and then create a document for the procedures manual that describes the formatting and conditions you applied to the forms in **5-LewisCenter.accdb**. Save the completed document and name it **5-Manual**. Print and then close **5-Manual.docx**.

Figure WB-5.2 Case Study Part 2

Patients Form		
Patient number 030 Rhonda J. Mahler 130 East 41st Street Tulsa, OK 74155 (918) 555-3107	Patient number 076 Patrick S. Robbins 3281 Aspen Avenue Tulsa, OK 74108 (918) 555-9672	Patient number 092 Oren L. Vargas 21320 Tenth Street Broken Arrow, OK 74012 (918) 555-1188
Patient number 085 Michael A. Dempsey 506 Houston Street Tulsa, OK 74142 (918) 555-5541	Patient number 074 Wendy L. Holloway 23849 22nd Street Broken Arrow, OK 74009 (918) 555-8842	Patient number 023 Maggie M. Winters 4422 South 121st Tulsa, OK 74142 (918) 555-8833
Doctors Form		
Doctor number 1 Carolyn Joswick (918) 555-4772	Doctor number 2 Gerald Ingram (918) 555-9890	Doctor number 3 Kay Feather (918) 555-7762
Doctor number 4 Sean Granger (918) 555-1039	Doctor number 5 Jerome Deltoro (918) 555-8021	
Services Form		
Co = Consultation C = Cataract Testing	V = Vision Screening S = Surgery	G = Glaucoma Testing E = Emergency
Billing Form		
Patient number 076 Doctor number 2 Date of visit = 4/1/2018 Service ID = C Fee = $85	Patient number 076 Doctor number 3 Date of visit = 4/1/2018 Service ID = V Fee = $150	Patient number 085 Doctor number 1 Date of visit = 4/1/2018 Service ID = Co Fee = $0
Patient number 074 Doctor number 3 Date of visit = 4/1/2018 Service ID = V Fee = $150	Patient number 023 Doctor number 5 Date of visit = 4/1/2018 Service ID = S Fee = $750	Patient number 092 Doctor number 1 Date of visit = 4/1/2018 Service ID = G Fee = $85

Microsoft® Access®

Creating Reports and Mailing Labels

Study tools include a presentation and a list of chapter Quick Steps and Hint margin notes. Use these resources to help you further develop and review skills learned in this chapter.

Concepts Check

SNAP Check your understanding by identifying application tools used in this chapter. If you are a SNAP user, launch the Concepts Check from your Assignments page.

Recheck

SNAP Check your understanding by taking this quiz. If you are a SNAP user, launch the Recheck from your Assignments page.

Skills Exercise

SNAP Additional activities are available to SNAP users. If you are a SNAP user, access these activities from your Assignments page.

Skills Assessment

Assessment

1

Data Files

Create and Format Reports in the Hilltop Database

1. Open **6-Hilltop.accdb** and enable the content.
2. Create a report with the Inventory table using the Report button.
3. With the report in Layout view, apply the following formatting:
   a. Center the data below each of the following column headings: *EquipmentID*, *AvailableHours*, *ServiceHours*, and *RepairHours*.
   b. Select all of the control objects and then change the font to Constantia.
   c. Select the objects containing currency amounts below the *PurchasePrice* column heading and then click the Decrease Decimals button (in the Number group) until the amounts display with no digits past the decimal point.
   d. Click in the *$473,260.00* amount and then click the Decrease Decimals button until the amount displays with no digits past the decimal point.
   e. Change the title of the report to *Inventory Report*.
4. Save the report with the name *InventoryReport*.
5. Print and then close InventoryReport.
6. Create a query in Design view with the following specifications:
   a. Add the Customers, Equipment, Invoices, and Rates tables to the query window.
   b. Insert the *Customer* field from the Customers table field list box in the first field in the *Field* row.
   c. Insert the *Equipment* field from the Equipment table field list box in the second field in the *Field* row.

d. Insert the *Hours* field from the Invoices table field list box in the third field in the *Field* row.

e. Insert the *Rate* field from the Rates table field list box in the fourth field in the *Field* row.

f. Click in the fifth field in the *Field* row, type Total:[Hours]*[Rate], and then press the Enter key.

g. Run the query.

h. Save the query with the name *CustomerRentals* and then close the query.

7. Create a report with the CustomerRentals query using the Report button.

8. With the report in Layout view, apply the following formatting:

a. Select the control objects containing currency amounts and then click the Decrease Decimals button until the amounts display with no digits past the decimal point.

b. Decrease the widths of the columns so the right border of each column displays near the right side of the longest entry.

c. Click in the *Total* column and then total the amounts by clicking the Report Layout Tools Design tab, clicking the Totals button in the Grouping & Totals group, and then clicking *Sum* at the drop-down list.

d. Click the total amount (at the bottom of the *Total* column), click the Report Layout Tools Format tab, and then click the Apply Currency Format button in the Number group.

e. Increase the height of the total amount row so the entire amount is visible.

f. Select and then delete the control object containing the amount that displays at the bottom of the *Rate* column.

g. Display the Group, Sort, and Total pane; group the records by *Customer*; sort by *Equipment*; and then close the pane.

h. Apply the Integral theme. (Do this with the Themes button in the Themes group on the Report Layout Tools Design tab.)

i. Select the five column headings and change the font color to standard black.

j. Change the title of the report to *Rentals*.

9. Save the report with the name *RentalReport*.

10. Print and then close RentalReport.

Assessment 2

Create Reports Using the Report Wizard

1. With **6-Hilltop.accdb** open, create a report using the Report Wizard with the following specifications:

a. At the first Report Wizard dialog box, insert the following fields in the *Selected Fields* list box:

From the Equipment table:	*Equipment*
From the Inventory table:	*PurchaseDate*
	PurchasePrice
	AvailableHours

b. Do not make any changes at the second Report Wizard dialog box.

c. Do not make any changes at the third Report Wizard dialog box.

d. At the fourth Report Wizard dialog box, choose the *Columnar* option.

e. At the fifth and last Report Wizard dialog box, click the Finish button. (This accepts the default report name *Equipment*.)

2. Print and then close the report.

3. Create a report using the Report Wizard with the following specifications:
   a. At the first Report Wizard dialog box, insert the following fields in the *Selected Fields* list box:

From the Customers table:	*Customer*
From the Invoices table:	*BillingDate*
	Hours
From the Equipment table:	*Equipment*
From the Rates table:	*Rate*

   b. Do not make any changes at the second Report Wizard dialog box.
   c. Do not make any changes at the third Report Wizard dialog box.
   d. Do not make any changes at the fourth Report Wizard dialog box.
   e. At the fifth Report Wizard dialog box, choose the *Block* option.
   f. At the sixth and last Report Wizard dialog box, name the report *Rentals*.
4. Print and then close the report.

Assessment 3

Create Mailing Labels

1. With **6-Hilltop.accdb** open, click the *Customers* table in the Tables group in the Navigation pane.
2. Use the Label Wizard to create mailing labels (you determine the label type) with customer names and addresses and sort the labels by customer names. Name the mailing label report *CustomerMailingLabels*.
3. Print the mailing labels.
4. Close the mailing labels report.

Assessment 4

Add a Field to a Report

1. In Chapter 5, you added a field to an existing form using the Field List task pane. Experiment with adding a field to an existing report and then complete the following:
   a. Open the RentalReport report (created in Assessment 1) in Layout view.
   b. Display the Field List task pane and display all of the tables.
   c. Drag the *BillingDate* field from the Invoices table so the field is positioned between the *Equipment* column and *Hours* column. At the message indicating that Access will modify the RecordSource property and asking if you want to continue, click Yes.
   d. Close the Field List task pane.
2. Save, print, and then close the report.
3. Close **6-Hilltop.accdb**.

Visual Benchmark

Design a Query and Create a Report with the Query

Data Files

1. Open **6-Skyline.accdb**, enable the content, and then create and run the query shown in Figure WB-6.1.
2. Save the query with the name *Suppliers2&4Orders* and then close the query.
3. Use the Report button to create the report shown in Figure WB-6.2 using the *Suppliers2&4Orders* query with the following specifications:
   a. Apply the Facet theme.
   b. Adjust the column widths and change the alignment of data as shown in Figure WB-6.2.

Figure WB-6.1 Visual Benchmark Query

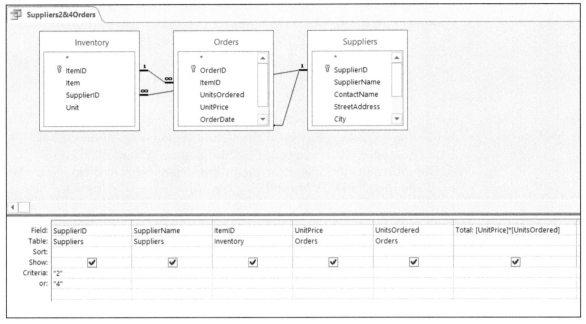

Field:	SupplierID	SupplierName	ItemID	UnitPrice	UnitsOrdered	Total: [UnitPrice]*[UnitsOrdered]
Table:	Suppliers	Suppliers	Inventory	Orders	Orders	
Sort:						
Show:	✓	✓	✓	✓	✓	✓
Criteria:	"2"					
or:	"4"					

Figure WB-6.2 Visual Benchmark Report

Suppliers 2 and 4 Orders					Friday, October 19, 2018 1:51:34 PM
SupplierID	SupplierName	ItemID	UnitPrice	UnitsOrdered	Total
2	Coral Produce	002	$10.50	3	$31.50
2	Coral Produce	016	$24.00	1	$24.00
4	Grocery Wholesalers	020	$18.75	2	$37.50
2	Coral Produce	014	$15.75	2	$31.50
4	Grocery Wholesalers	025	$28.50	1	$28.50
4	Grocery Wholesalers	036	$17.00	2	$34.00
4	Grocery Wholesalers	013	$14.00	2	$28.00
2	Coral Produce	004	$10.95	2	$21.90
4	Grocery Wholesalers	035	$17.00	1	$17.00
4	Grocery Wholesalers	027	$22.00	1	$22.00
4	Grocery Wholesalers	026	$29.25	1	$29.25
2	Coral Produce	021	$31.00	1	$31.00
4	Grocery Wholesalers	034	$13.75	2	$27.50
4	Grocery Wholesalers	012	$30.25	1	$30.25
4	Grocery Wholesalers	018	$45.00	1	$45.00
2	Coral Produce	016	$39.40	2	$78.80
4	Grocery Wholesalers	035	$17.00	1	$17.00
2	Coral Produce	014	$15.75	2	$31.50
4	Grocery Wholesalers	020	$18.75	2	$37.50
					$603.70

c. Change the title as shown in Figure WB-6.2.

d. Select the column headings and then apply the standard black font color.

e. Insert the total of the amounts in the *Total* column. Format the total amount as shown in Figure WB-6.2.

f. Delete the control object containing the sum amount at the bottom of the *UnitPrice* column.

4. Save the report with the name *Suppliers2&4OrdersRpt*.

5. Print the report, close the report, and then close **6-Skyline.accdb**.

Case Study

Part 1

Data Files

As the office manager at Millstone Legal Services, you need to enter records for three new clients in **6-Millstone.accdb**. Open **6-Millstone.accdb** and enable the content. Using the following information, enter the data in the appropriate tables:

Client number 42
Martin Costanzo
1002 Thomas Drive
Casper, WY 82602
(307) 555-5001
Mr. Costanzo saw Douglas Sheehan regarding divorce proceedings with a billing date of 3/15/2018 and a fee of $150.

Client number 43
Susan Nordyke
23193 Ridge Circle East
Mills, WY 82644
(307) 555-2719
Ms. Nordyke saw Loretta Ryder regarding support enforcement with a billing date of 3/15/2018 and a fee of $175.

Client number 44
Monica Sommers
1105 Riddell Avenue
Casper, WY 82609
(307) 555-1188
Ms. Sommers saw Anita Leland regarding a guardianship with a billing date of 3/15/2018 and a fee of $250.

Part 2

Create and print the following reports, queries, and labels:

• Create a report with the Clients table and the name *ClientRpt*. Apply formatting to enhance the appearance of the report.

• Create a query that displays the client ID, first name and last name, attorney last name, billing date, and fee. Name the query *ClientBilling*.

• Create a report with the ClientBilling query and name the report *ClientBillingRpt*. Group the records in the report by attorney last name (the *LName* field in the drop-down list) and sort alphabetically in ascending order by client last name (the *LastName* field in the drop-down list). Apply formatting to enhance the appearance of the report.

• Produce a telephone directory by creating a report named *ClientDirectory* that includes client last names, first names, and telephone numbers. Sort the records in the report alphabetically by last name in ascending order.

• Edit the ClientBilling query so it includes a criterion that displays only billing dates between 3/12/2018 and 3/15/2018. Save the query with Save Object As and name it *ClientBilling12-15*.

• Create a report with the ClientBilling12-15 query and the name *Billing12-15*. Apply formatting to enhance the appearance of the report.

• Create mailing labels for the clients and name the labels report *ClientLabels*.

Part 3

Apply the following conditions to fields in reports and then print the reports:

- In the ClientRpt report, apply the condition that the city *Casper* displays in the standard red font color and the city *Mills* displays the standard blue font color in the *City* field.

- In the ClientBillingRpt report, apply the condition that fees over $199 display in the standard green font color and fees less than $200 display in the standard blue font color.

Part 4

Your center has a manual that describes processes and procedures in the workplace. Open Word and create a document for the manual that describes how to create a report using the Report button and Report Wizard and how to create mailing labels using the Label Wizard. Save the completed document and name it **6-Manual**. Print and then close **6-Manual.docx**.

Modifying, Filtering, and Viewing Data

Study Tools

Study tools include a presentation and a list of chapter Quick Steps and Hint margin notes. Use these resources to help you further develop and review skills learned in this chapter.

Concepts Check

Check your understanding by identifying application tools used in this chapter. If you are a SNAP user, launch the Concepts Check from your Assignments page.

Recheck

Check your understanding by taking this quiz. If you are a SNAP user, launch the Recheck from your Assignments page.

Skills Exercise

Additional activities are available to SNAP users. If you are a SNAP user, access these activities from your Assignments page.

Skills Assessment

Assessment

1

Filter Records in Tables

1. Open **7-WarrenLegal.accdb** and enable the content.
2. Open the Clients table and then filter the records to display the following records:
   a. Display only those records of clients who live in Renton. When the records of clients in Renton display, print the results in landscape orientation and then remove the filter. *Hint: Change to landscape orientation in Print Preview.*
   b. Display only those records of clients with the zip code of 98033. When the records of clients with the zip code 98033 display, print the results in landscape orientation and then remove the filter.
3. Close the Clients table without saving the changes.
4. Open the Billing table and then filter the records by selection to display the following records:
   a. Display only those records with a category of *CC*. Print the records and then remove the filter.
   b. Display only those records with an attorney ID of *12*. Print the records and then remove the filter.
   c. Display only those records with dates between 6/1/2018 and 6/10/2018. Print the records and then remove the filter.
5. Close the Billing table without saving the changes.
6. Open the Clients table and then use the *Filter By Form* option to display clients in Auburn or Renton. (Be sure to use the Or tab at the bottom of the table.) Print the table in landscape orientation and then remove the filter.
7. Close the Clients table without saving the changes.

8. Open the Billing table and then use the *Filter By Form* option to display category G or P. Print the table and then remove the filter.
9. Close the Billing table without saving the changes.
10. Close **7-WarrenLegal.accdb**.

Assessment

2

Data Files

Set and Remove a Password; Save a Table and Database in Different File Formats

1. Open **7-Hilltop.accdb** in Exclusive mode and enable the content.
2. Create a password for the database (you determine the password), and with the Set Database Password dialog box open, create a screen capture of the dialog box by completing the following steps:
   a. Press the Alt + Print Screen buttons on your keyboard.
   b. Open a blank document in Microsoft Word.
   c. Click the Paste button in the Clipboard group on the Home tab. (This pastes the screen capture image in the Word document.)
   d. Click the File tab, click the *Print* option, and then click the Print button at the Print backstage area.
   e. Close Word by clicking the Close button in the upper right corner of the screen. At the message asking if you want to save the document, click the Don't Save button.
3. Click OK to close the Set Database Password dialog box.
4. At the message stating that a block cipher is incompatible with row level locking, click OK.
5. Close the database.
6. Open **7-Hilltop.accdb** in Exclusive mode and enter the password when prompted.
7. Remove the password. ***Hint: Do this with the Decrypt Database button in the Info backstage area***.
8. Open the Invoices table and then save the table in PDF file format with the default file name. Specify that you want the object to open when published.
9. When the table opens in Adobe Acrobat Reader, print the table by clicking the Print button in the upper left side of the screen and then clicking OK at the Print dialog box. (If the Print button is not visible, click the File option, click *Print* at the drop-down list, and then click OK at the Print dialog box.)
10. Close Adobe Acrobat Reader and then close the Invoices table.
11. Save **7-Hilltop.accdb** in the *Access 2002-2003 Database (*.mdb)* file format.
12. With the database open, make a screen capture using the Print Screen key on the keyboard. Open Word, paste the screen capture image in the Word document, print the document, and then close Word without saving the changes.
13. Close the database.

Assessment

3

Data Files

Delete and Rename Objects

1. Open **7-Hilltop.accdb**. (Make sure you open the 7-Hilltop database with the .accdb file extension.)
2. Right-click an object in the Navigation pane, experiment with options in the shortcut menu, and then complete these steps using the shortcut menu:
   a. Delete the Inventory form.
   b. Change the name of the Equipment form to *EquipForm*.
   c. Change the name of the InvReport report to *InventoryReport*.

d. Export (using the shortcut menu) the EquipmentQuery query to a Word RTF file. *Hint: Click the Browse button at the Export - RTF File dialog box.*

e. Open the **EquipmentQuery.rtf** file in Word, print the file, and then close Word.

3. Close **7-Hilltop.accdb**.

Visual Benchmark

Data Files

Design a Query and Filter the Query

1. Open **7-PacTrek.accdb** and enable the content.
2. Create and run the query shown in Figure WB-7.1.
3. Save the query with the name *ProductsOnOrder*.
4. Print the query.
5. Filter the query so the records display as shown in Figure WB-7.2. *Hint: Filter the supplier names as shown in Figure WB-7.2 and then filter the UnitsOnOrder field to show records that do not equal 0.*
6. Print the filtered query.
7. Remove the filters and then close the query without saving the changes.
8. Close **7-PacTrek.accdb**.

Figure WB-7.1 Visual Benchmark Query

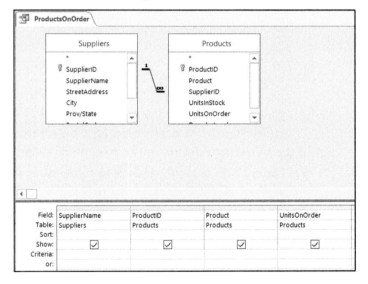

Figure WB-7.2 Visual Benchmark Filtered Query

SupplierName	ProductID	Product	UnitsOnOrder
Hopewell, Inc.	152-H	Lantern hanger	15
Hopewell, Inc.	155-20	Shursite angle-head flashlight	20
Hopewell, Inc.	155-35	Shursite portable camp light	10
Cascade Gear	250-L	Cascade R4 jacket, ML	10
Cascade Gear	250-XL	Cascade R4 jacket, MXL	10
Cascade Gear	255-M	Cascade R4 jacket, WM	5
Cascade Gear	255-XL	Cascade R4 jacket, WXL	5

Case Study

As the office manager at Summit View Medical Services, you are responsible for maintaining clinic records. Open **7-SummitView.accdb**, enable the content, and then insert the following additional services into the appropriate table:

- Edit the *Doctor visit* entry in the Services table so it displays as *Clinic visit*.
- Add the entry *X-ray* with a service identification of *X*.
- Add the entry *Cholesterol screening* with a service identification of *CS*.

Add the following new patient information in the database in the appropriate tables:

Patient number 121
Brian M. Gould
2887 Nelson Street
Helena, MT 59604
(406) 555-3121
Mr. Gould saw Dr. Wallace for a clinic visit on 4/5/2018, which has a fee of $75.

Patient number 122
Ellen L. Augustine
12990 148th Street
East Helena, MT 59635
(406) 555-0722
Ms. Augustine saw Dr. Kennedy for cholesterol screening on 4/5/2018, which has a fee of $90.

Patient number 123
Jeff J. Masura
3218 Eldridge Avenue
Helena, MT 59624
(406) 555-6212
Mr. Masura saw Dr. Rowe for an x-ray on 4/5/2018, which has a fee of $75.

Add the following information to the Billing table:

- Patient 109 came for cholesterol screening with Dr. Kennedy on 4/6/2018 with a $90 fee.
- Patient 106 came for immunizations with Dr. Pena on 4/6/2018 with a $100 fee.
- Patient 114 came for an x-ray with Dr. Kennedy on 4/6/2018 with a $75 fee.

Create the following filters and queries:

- Open the Billing table and then filter and print the records for the date 4/2/2018. Clear the filter and then filter and print the records with a doctor number of 18. Clear the filter and then save and close the table.
- Create a report that displays the patient's first name, last name, street address, city, state, and zip code. Apply formatting to enhance the appearance of the report. Filter and print the records of those patients living in Helena, remove the filter, and then filter and print the records of those patients living in East Helena. Save and then close the report.

- Design a query that includes the doctor number, doctor last name, patient number, date of visit, and fee. Save the query with the name *DoctorBillingFees* and then print the query. Filter and print the records for Dr. Kennedy and Dr. Pena, remove the filter, and then filter and print the records for the dates 4/5/2018 and 4/6/2018. Save and then close the query.

Part 3

You want to make the Billing table available for viewing on computers without Access, so you decide to save the table in PDF file format. Save the Billing table in PDF file format, print the table in Adobe Acrobat Reader, and then close Adobe Acrobat Reader. Close **7-SummitView.accdb**.

Part 4

Your clinic has a manual that describes processes and procedures in the workplace. Open Word and then create a document for the manual that describes the steps you followed to create the DoctorBillingFees query and to create and print the two filters. Save the completed document and name it **7-Manual**. Print and then close **7-Manual.docx**.

Exporting and Importing Data

Study tools include a presentation and a list of chapter Quick Steps and Hint margin notes. Use these resources to help you further develop and review skills learned in this chapter.

Concepts Check

Check your understanding by identifying application tools used in this chapter. If you are a SNAP user, launch the Concepts Check from your Assignments page.

Recheck

Check your understanding by taking this quiz. If you are a SNAP user, launch the Recheck from your Assignments page.

Skills Exercise

Additional activities are available to SNAP users. If you are a SNAP user, access these activities from your Assignments page.

Skills Assessment

Assessment

1

Data Files

Export a Form to Excel and a Report to Word

1. Open **8-WarrenLegal.accdb** and enable the content.
2. Create a form named *Billing* using the Form Wizard with the following fields:

   From the Billing table: *BillingID*
                                       ClientID
                                       BillingDate
                                       Hours

   From the Rates table: *Rate*

3. When the form displays, close it.
4. Export the Billing form to an Excel worksheet and specify that the Excel file should open after the export operation is complete.
5. Make the following changes to the Excel Billing worksheet:
   a. Select columns A through E and then adjust the column widths.
   b. Select the range A2:B42 and then click the Center button in the Alignment group on the Home tab.
   c. Save the Billing worksheet.
   d. Print and then close the Billing worksheet.
   e. Close Excel.
6. In Access, close the dialog box.

7. Create a report named *ClientBilling* using the Report Wizard (at the fifth wizard dialog box, change the layout to *Block*) with the following fields:

    From the Clients table: *FirstName*
                              LastName

    From the Billing table: *BillingDate*
                              Hours

    From the Rates table: *Rate*

8. Close the report.
9. Create a Word document with the ClientBilling report and save it with the default name. In the Word document, make the following changes:
   a. Press Ctrl + A to select the entire document, change the font color to Black, and then deselect the text.
   b. Insert a space between *Client* and *Billing* in the title.
   c. Position the insertion point immediately right of the word *Billing*, press the spacebar, and then type of Legal Services.
10. Save and then print **ClientBilling.rtf**.
11. Close the document and then close Word.
12. In Access, close the dialog box.

Merge Table and Query Data with a Word Document

Assessment 2

1. With **8-WarrenLegal.accdb** open, merge data in the Clients table with a new Word document using the Word Merge button.
2. Maximize the Word document, close the Mail Merge task pane, and then compose a letter with the following elements:
   a. Click the Home tab and then click the *No Spacing* style in the Styles group.
   b. Press the Enter key six times, type the current date, and then press the Enter key four times.
   c. Click the Mailings tab and then insert the «AddressBlock» composite field.
   d. Press the Enter key two times and then type the salutation Ladies and Gentlemen:.
   e. Press the Enter key two times and then type the following text (press the Enter key two times after typing the first paragraph of text):

   > The last time you visited our offices, you may have noticed how crowded we were. To alleviate the overcrowding, we are leasing new offices in the Meridian Building and will be moving in at the beginning of next month.
   >
   > Stop by and see our new offices at our open house planned for the second Friday of next month. Drop by any time between 2:00 and 5:30 p.m. We look forward to seeing you.

   f. After typing the second paragraph, press the Enter key two times, type Sincerely, and then press the Enter key four times. Type Marjorie Shaw, press the Enter key, and then type Senior Partner. Press the Enter key two times, type your initials, press the Enter key, and then type 8-WLLtrs.docx.
3. Merge to a new document and then save the document and name it **8-WLLtrs**.
4. Print only the first two letters in the document and then close **8-WLLtrs.docx**.
5. Save the main document and name it **8-WLLtrMD1**. Close the document and then close Word.
6. With **8-WarrenLegal.accdb** open, extract the records from the Clients table of those clients located in Kent and then name the query *ClientsKent*. (Include all of the fields from the table in the query.)

7. Merge the ClientsKent query to a new Word document using the Word Merge button.
8. Maximize the Word document, close the Mail Merge task pane, and then compose a letter with the following elements:
   a. Click the Home tab and then click the *No Spacing* style in the Styles group.
   b. Press the Enter key six times, type the current date, and then press the Enter key four times.
   c. Click the Mailings tab and then insert the «AddressBlock» composite field.
   d. Insert a proper salutation (refer to step 2d).
   e. Compose a letter to clients that includes the following information:

   > The City of Kent Municipal Court has moved from 1024 Meeker Street to a new building located at 3201 James Avenue. All court hearings after the end of this month will be held at the new address. If you need directions to the new building, please call our office.

   f. Include an appropriate complimentary close for the letter (refer to Step 2f). Use the name *Thomas Zeiger* and the title *Attorney* in the complimentary close and add your reference initials and the document name (**8-WLKentLtrs.docx**).
9. Merge the letter to a new document and then save the document and name it **8-WLKentLtrs**.
10. Print only the first two letters in the document and then close **8-WLKentLtrs.docx**.
11. Save the main document and name it **8-WLLtrMD2**, close the document, and then close Word.

<table>
<tr><td>Assessment
3

</td><td>

Link an Excel Workbook

1. With **8-WarrenLegal.accdb** open, link **8-Cases.xlsx** into a new table named *Cases*.
2. Open the Cases table in Datasheet view.
3. Print and then close the Cases table.
4. Open Excel, open **8-Cases.xlsx**, and then add the following data in the specified cells:

</td></tr>
</table>

A8	57-D
B8	130
C8	1100
A9	42-A
B9	144
C9	3250
A10	29-C
B10	125
C10	900

5. Save, print, and then close **8-Cases.xlsx**.
6. Close Excel.
7. In Access, open the Cases table in Datasheet view. (Notice the changes you made in Excel are reflected in the table.)
8. Print and then close the Cases table.
9. Close **8-WarrenLegal.accdb**.

Visual Benchmark

Create a Report and Export the Report to Word

Data Files

1. Open **8-Dearborn.accdb** and enable the content.
2. Use the Report Wizard to create the report shown in Figure WB-8.1. (Use the Quotas table and Representatives table when creating the report and choose the *Block* layout at the fifth wizard dialog box.) Save the report with the name *RepQuotas* and then print the report.
3. Use the RepQuotas report and export it to Word. Format the report in Word as shown in Figure WB-8.2. Print the Word document and then close Word.
4. In Access, close **8-Dearborn.accdb**.

Figure WB-8.1 Visual Benchmark Report

RepQuotas

Quota	RepName	Telephone
$100,000.00	Robin Rehberg	(317) 555-9812
	Andre Kulisek	(317) 555-2264
	Edward Harris	(317) 555-3894
	Cecilia Ortega	(317) 555-4810
$150,000.00	David DeBruler	(317) 555-8779
	Jaren Newman	(317) 555-6790
	Lee Hutchinson	(765) 555-4277
	Craig Johnson	(317) 555-4391
$200,000.00	Isabelle Marshall	(765) 555-8822
	Maureen Pascual	(317) 555-5513
	Linda Foster	(317) 555-2101
	Catherine Singleton	(317) 555-0172
$250,000.00	Kwan Im	(317) 555-8374
	William Ludlow	(317) 555-0991
	Lydia Alvarado	(765) 555-4996
$300,000.00	Gina Tapparo	(317) 555-0044
	Alfred Silva	(317) 555-3211

Figure WB-8.2 Visual Benchmark Word Document

Representatives' Quotas

Quota	RepName	Telephone
$100,000.00	Robin Rehberg	(317) 555-9812
	Andre Kulisek	(317) 555-2264
	Edward Harris	(317) 555-3894
	Cecilia Ortega	(317) 555-4810
$150,000.00	David DeBruler	(317) 555-8779
	Jaren Newman	(317) 555-6790
	Lee Hutchinson	(765) 555-4277
	Craig Johnson	(317) 555-4391
$200,000.00	Isabelle Marshall	(765) 555-8822
	Maureen Pascual	(317) 555-5513
	Linda Foster	(317) 555-2101
	Catherine Singleton	(317) 555-0172
$250,000.00	Kwan Im	(317) 555-8374
	William Ludlow	(317) 555-0991
	Lydia Alvarado	(765) 555-4996
$300,000.00	Gina Tapparo	(317) 555-0044
	Alfred Silva	(317) 555-3211

Case Study

As the office manager at Woodland Dermatology Center, you are responsible for managing the center's database. In preparation for an upcoming meeting, open **8-Woodland.accdb** and prepare the following using data in the database:

- Create a query that displays the patient identification number, first name, and last name; doctor last name; date of visit; and fee. Name the query *PatientBilling*.
- Export the PatientBilling query to an Excel worksheet. Apply formatting to enhance the appearance of the worksheet and then print the worksheet.
- Create mailing labels for the patients. *Hint: Use the Labels button on the Create tab*.
- Export the patient labels to a Word (.rtf) document and then print the document.
- Import and link the Excel worksheet named **8-Payroll.xlsx** to a new table named *WeeklyPayroll*. Print the WeeklyPayroll table.

You have been given some updated information about the weekly payroll and need to make the following changes to **8-Payroll.xlsx**:

- Change the hours for Irene Vaughn to *30*
- Change the wage for Monica Saunders to *$10.50*
- Change the hours for Dale Jorgensen to *20*.

After making and saving the changes, open, print, and then close the WeeklyPayroll table. Close **8-Payroll.xlsx**.

Part

2

The center is expanding and will be offering cosmetic dermatology services at the beginning of next month to residents in the Altoona area. Design a query that extracts records of patients living in the city of Altoona and then merge the query with Word. Write a letter in the Word document describing the new services, which include microdermabrasion, chemical peels, laser resurfacing, sclerotherapy, and photorejuvenation, as well as an offer for a free facial and consultation. *Note that since the letter is from you as the author, you do not need to include reference initials.* Insert the appropriate fields in the document and then complete the merge. Save the merged document and name it **8-WLDLtrs**. Print the first two letters of the document and then close the document. Close the main document without saving it and then close Word.

Part

3

The Woodland database contains critical information and you need to determine how often you should back up the database. (You learned how to back up a database in Chapter 7.) Use Access Help to learn more about the backup process and, more specifically, about guidelines for when to back up a database. Search Access Help for the article <u>Compact and repair database files</u>. Click the hyperlink to the article (be sure to click the hyperlink to the article with the exact title). Scroll down the article and then click the hyperlink <u>protect data with backup and restore processes</u> that displays in the sentence *For more information about how to protect data with backup and restore processes*. Read the hyperlinked article <u>Protect your data with backup and restore processes</u>. Since you are responsible for updating the clinic procedures manual, create a Word document that describes how often you think the Woodland database should be backed up and the rationale behind your backup plan. Include steps for creating a backup of the database. Save the completed document and name it **8-Manual**. Print and then close **8-Manual.docx**.

Unit 2 Performance Assessment

Data Files

Before beginning unit work, copy the AL1U2 folder to your storage medium and then make AL1U2 the active folder.

Assessing Proficiency

In this unit, you have learned to create forms, reports, and mailing labels and filter data. You have also learned how to modify document properties; view object dependencies; and export, import, and link data between programs.

Assessment

1

Create Tables in a Clinic Database

1. Use Access to create a database for clients of a mental health clinic. Name the database **U2-LancasterClinic**. Create a table named *Clients* that includes the fields listed below. (You determine the field name, data type, field size, and description.)

> *ClientNumber* (primary key field)
> *ClientName*
> *StreetAddress*
> *City*
> *State*
> *ZipCode*
> *Telephone*
> *DateOfBirth*
> *DiagnosisID*

2. After creating the table, switch to Datasheet view and then enter the following data in the appropriate fields:

ClientNumber	1831	*ClientNumber*	3219
ClientName	George Charoni	*ClientName*	Marian Wilke
StreetAddress	3980 Broad Street	*StreetAddress*	12032 South 39th
City	Philadelphia	*City*	Jenkintown
State	PA	*State*	PA
ZipCode	19149	*ZipCode*	19209
Telephone	(215) 555-3482	*Telephone*	(215) 555-9083
DateOfBirth	4/12/1964	*DateOfBirth*	10/23/1987
DiagnosisID	SC	*DiagnosisID*	OCD

ClientNumber	2874	ClientNumber	5831
ClientName	Arthur Shroeder	ClientName	Roshawn Collins
StreetAddress	3618 Fourth Avenue	StreetAddress	12110 52nd Court East
City	Philadelphia	City	Cheltenham
State	PA	State	PA
ZipCode	19176	ZipCode	19210
Telephone	(215) 555-8311	Telephone	(215) 555-4770
DateOfBirth	3/23/1964	DateOfBirth	11/3/1971
DiagnosisID	OCD	DiagnosisID	SC

ClientNumber	4419	ClientNumber	1103
ClientName	Lorena Hearron	ClientName	Raymond Mandato
StreetAddress	3112 96th Street East	StreetAddress	631 Garden Boulevard
City	Philadelphia	City	Jenkintown
State	PA	State	PA
ZipCode	19132	ZipCode	19209
Telephone	(215) 555-3281	Telephone	(215) 555-0957
DateOfBirth	7/2/1990	DateOfBirth	9/20/1985
DiagnosisID	AD	DiagnosisID	MDD

3. Automatically adjust the column widths.
4. Save, print, and then close the Clients table.
5. Create a table named *Diagnoses* that includes the following fields:

   DiagnosisID (primary key field)
   Diagnosis

6. After creating the table, switch to Datasheet view and then enter the following data in the appropriate fields:

DiagnosisID	AD
Diagnosis	Adjustment Disorder

DiagnosisID	MDD
Diagnosis	Manic-Depressive Disorder

DiagnosisID	OCD
Diagnosis	Obsessive-Compulsive Disorder

DiagnosisID	SC
Diagnosis	Schizophrenia

7. Automatically adjust the column widths.
8. Save, print, and then close the Diagnoses table.
9. Create a table named *Fees* that includes the fields listed below. (You determine the field name, data type, field size, and description.)

   FeeCode (primary key field)
   HourlyFee

10. After creating the table, switch to Datasheet view and then enter the following data in the appropriate fields:

FeeCode	A	*FeeCode*	E
HourlyFee	$75.00	*HourlyFee*	$95.00
FeeCode	B	*FeeCode*	F
HourlyFee	$80.00	*HourlyFee*	$100.00
FeeCode	C	*FeeCode*	G
HourlyFee	$85.00	*HourlyFee*	$105.00
FeeCode	D	*FeeCode*	H
HourlyFee	$90.00	*HourlyFee*	$110.00

11. Automatically adjust the column widths.
12. Save, print, and then close the Fees table.
13. Create a table named *Employees* that includes the fields listed below. (You determine the field name, data type, field size, and description.)

> *ProviderNumber* (primary key field)
> *ProviderName*
> *Title*
> *Extension*

14. After creating the table, switch to Datasheet view and then enter the following data in the appropriate fields:

ProviderNumber	29	*ProviderNumber*	15
ProviderName	James Schouten	*ProviderName*	Lynn Yee
Title	Psychologist	*Title*	Child Psychologist
Extension:	399	*Extension*	102
ProviderNumber	33	*ProviderNumber*	18
ProviderName	Janice Grisham	*ProviderName*	Craig Chilton
Title	Psychiatrist	*Title*	Psychologist
Extension	11	*Extension*	20

15. Automatically adjust the column widths.
16. Save, print, and then close the Employees table.
17. Create a table named *Billing* that includes the fields listed below. (You determine the field name, data type, field size, and description.)

> *BillingNumber* (primary key field; apply the AutoNumber data type)
> *ClientNumber*
> *DateOfService* (apply the Date/Time data type)
> *Insurer*
> *ProviderNumber*
> *Hours* (Apply the Number data type, change the *Field Size* option in the *Field Properties* section to *Double*, and the *Decimal Places* option in the *Field Properties* section in Design view to *1*. Two of the records will contain a number requiring this format.)
> *FeeCode*

18. After creating the table, switch to Datasheet view and then enter the following data in the appropriate fields:

ClientNumber	4419	*ClientNumber*	1831
DateOfService	3/5/2018	*DateOfService*	3/5/2018
Insurer	Health Plus	*Insurer*	Self
ProviderNumber	15	*ProviderNumber*	33
Hours	2	*Hours*	1
FeeCode	B	*FeeCode*	H
ClientNumber	3219	*ClientNumber*	5831
DateOfService	3/6/2018	*DateOfService*	3/6/2018
Insurer	Health Plus	*Insurer*	Penn-State Health
ProviderNumber	15	*ProviderNumber*	18
Hours	1	*Hours*	2
FeeCode	D	*FeeCode*	C
ClientNumber	4419	*ClientNumber*	1103
DateOfService	3/7/2018	*DateOfService*	3/7/2018
Insurer	Health Plus	*Insurer*	Penn-State Health
ProviderNumber	15	*ProviderNumber*	18
Hours	1	*Hours*	0.5
FeeCode	A	*FeeCode*	A
ClientNumber	1831	*ClientNumber*	5831
DateOfService	3/8/2018	*DateOfService*	3/8/2018
Insurer	Self	*Insurer*	Penn-State Health
ProviderNumber	33	*ProviderNumber:*	18
Hours	1	*Hours*	0.5
FeeCode	H	*FeeCode*	C

19. Automatically adjust the column widths.
20. Save, print in landscape orientation, and then close the Billing table.

Assessment 2

Relate Tables and Create Forms in a Clinic Database

1. With **U2-LancasterClinic.accdb** open, create the following one-to-many relationships and enforce referential integrity and cascade fields and records:
   a. *ClientNumber* in the Clients table is the "one" and *ClientNumber* in the Billing table is the "many."
   b. *DiagnosisID* in the Diagnoses table is the "one" and *DiagnosisID* in the Clients table is the "many."
   c. *ProviderNumber* in the Employees table is the "one" and *ProviderNumber* in the Billing table is the "many."
   d. *FeeCode* in the Fees table is the "one" and *FeeCode* in the Billing table is the "many."
2. Create a form with the data in the Clients table.

3. After creating the form, add the following record to the Clients form:

ClientNumber	1179
ClientName	Timothy Fierro
StreetAddress	1133 Tenth Southwest
City	Philadelphia
State	PA
ZipCode	19178
Telephone	(215) 555-5594
DateOfBirth	12/7/1993
DiagnosisID	AD

4. Save the form with the default name, print the form in landscape orientation, and then close the form.
5. Add the following records to the Billing table:

ClientNumber	1179	*ClientNumber*	1831
DateOfService	3/8/2018	*DateOfService*	3/8/2018
Insurer	Health Plus	*Insurer*	Self
ProviderNumber	15	*ProviderNumber*	33
Hours	0.5	*Hours*	1
FeeCode	C	*FeeCode*	H

6. Print the Billing table in landscape orientation.
7. Close the Billing table.

Assessment 3

Create Forms Using the Form Wizard

1. With **U2-LancasterClinic.accdb** open, create a form with fields from related tables using the Form Wizard with the following specifications:
   a. At the first Form Wizard dialog box, insert the following fields in the *Selected Fields* list box:

   From the Clients table: *ClientNumber*
   DateOfBirth
   DiagnosisID

   From the Billing table: *Insurer*
   ProviderNumber

   b. Do not make any changes at the second Form Wizard dialog box.
   c. Do not make any changes at the third Form Wizard dialog box.
   d. At the fourth Form Wizard dialog box, type the name ProviderInformation in the *Form* text box, and then finish the Form Wizard.
2. When the first record displays, print the first record.
3. Close the form.

Assessment 4

Create Labels with the Label Wizard

1. With **U2-LancasterClinic.accdb** open, use the Label Wizard to create mailing labels with the client names and addresses and sort by zip code. Name the mailing label report *ClientMailingLabels*.
2. Print the mailing labels.
3. Close the mailing labels report.

Assessment 5

Filter Records in Tables

1. With **U2-LancasterClinic.accdb** open, open the Billing table and then filter the records to display the following records:
   a. Display only those records with the Health Plus insurer. Print the results in landscape orientation and then remove the filter.
   b. Display only those records with a client number of 4419. Print the results and then remove the filter.
2. Filter records by selection to display the following records:
   a. Display only those records with a fee code of C. Print the results and then remove the filter.
   b. Display only those records between the dates of 3/5/2018 and 3/7/2018. Print the results and then remove the filter.
3. Close the Billing table without saving the changes.
4. Open the Clients table and then use the *Filter By Form* option to display clients in Jenkintown or Cheltenham. Print the results in landscape orientation and then remove the filter.
5. Close the Clients table without saving the changes.

Assessment 6

Export a Table to Excel

1. With **U2-LancasterClinic.accdb** open, export the Billing table to an Excel workbook to your AL1U2 folder.
2. Apply formatting to the cells in the Excel workbook to enhance the appearance of the data.
3. Change to landscape orientation.
4. Save, print, and then close the workbook.
5. Close Excel.

Assessment 7

Merge Records to Create Letters in Word

1. With **U2-LancasterClinic.accdb** open, merge data in the Clients table to a blank Word document. ***Hint: Use the Word Merge button in the Export group on the External Data tab.*** At the Word document, click the Home tab and then click the *No Spacing* style. Press the Enter key six times, type March 12, 2018, press the Enter key four times, and then insert fields for the inside address (you cannot use the *AddressBlock* field). Press the Enter key two times after the fields for the inside address, type an appropriate salutation, press the Enter key two times, and then type the letter with the following text in the body of the document:

   The building of a new wing for the Lancaster Clinic will begin April 1, 2018. We are excited about this new addition to our clinic. With the new facilities, we will be able to offer additional community and group services along with enhanced child-play therapy treatment.

   During the construction, the main entrance will be moved to the north end of the building. Please use this entrance until the construction of the wing is completed. We apologize in advance for any inconvenience this causes you.

   Include an appropriate complimentary close for the letter. Use the name and title *Marianne Lambert, Clinic Director* for the signature and add your reference initials and the document name (**U2-LCLtrs.docx**).

2. Merge to a new document and then save the document and name it **U2-LCLtrs**.
3. Print the first two letters of the document and then close **U2-LCLtrs.docx**.
4. Save the main document and name it **U2-ConstLtrMD**.
5. Close the document and then close Word.

Assessment

8

Import and Link Excel Data to an Access Table

1. With **U2-LancasterClinic.accdb** open, import and link **U2-StaffHours.xlsx** to a new table named *StaffHours*.
2. Open the StaffHours table in Datasheet view.
3. Print and then close the StaffHours table.
4. Open **U2-StaffHours.xlsx** in Excel.
5. Insert a formula in cell D2 that multiplies B2 by C2 and then copy the formula down to the range D3:D7.
6. Save and then close **U2-StaffHours.xlsx**.
7. Close Excel.
8. In Access with **U2-LancasterClinic.accdb** open, open the StaffHours table.
9. Print and then close the StaffHours table.

Writing Activities

The following activities give you the opportunity to practice your writing skills while you demonstrate your understanding of some of the important Access features you have mastered in this unit. Use correct grammar, appropriate word choices, and clear sentence constructions.

Activity

1

Add a Table to the Clinic Database

The director at Lancaster Clinic has asked you to add information to **U2-LancasterClinic.accdb** on insurance companies contracted by the clinic. To do so, you will need to create a table that will contain information on insurance companies. The director wants the table to include the insurance company name, address, city, state, and zip code, along with the telephone number and name of the company representative. You determine the field names, data types, field sizes, and description for the table and then include the following information (in the appropriate fields):

Health Plus
4102 22nd Street
Philadelphia, PA 19166
(212) 555-0990
Representative: Byron Tolleson

Penn-State Health
5933 Lehigh Avenue
Philadelphia, PA 19148
(212) 555-3477
Representative: Tracey Pavone

Quality Medical
51 Cecil B Moore Avenue
Philadelphia, PA 19168
(212) 555-4600
Representative: Lee Stafford

Delaware Health
4418 Front Street
Philadelphia, PA 19132
(212) 555-6770
Representative: Melanie Chon

Save the insurance company table, print it in landscape orientation, and then close the table. Open Word and then write a report to the clinic director detailing how you created the table. Include a title for the report, steps on how you created the table, and any other pertinent information. Save the completed report with the name **U2-LCRpt**. Print and then close **U2-LCRpt.docx**.

Activity
2

Merge Records to Create Letters to Insurance Companies

Merge data in the insurance company database to a blank Word document. You determine the fields to use in the inside address (you cannot use the Address Block button) and an appropriate salutation. Compose a letter to the insurance companies informing them that Lancaster Clinic is providing mental health counseling services to people who have health insurance through their employers. You are sending an informational brochure about Lancaster Clinic and are requesting information from the insurance companies on services and service limitations. Include an appropriate complimentary close for the letter. Use the name and title *Marianne Lambert, Clinic Director* for the signature and add your reference initials. When the merge is completed, name the document containing the merged letters **U2-LCIns**. Print the first two letters in the merged document and then close **U2-LCIns.docx**. Close the main document without saving it and then close Word. Close **U2-LancasterClinic.accdb**.

Internet Research

Health Information Search

Search the Internet for information on a health concern or disease that interests you. Look for specific organizations, interest groups, or individuals who are somehow connected to the topic you have chosen. You may find information about an organization that raises money to support research, a support group that posts information or answers questions, or clinics or doctors that specialize in your topic. Try to find at least 10 different organizations, groups, or individuals that support the health concern you are researching.

Create a database in Access and then create a table that includes information from your research. Design the table so that you can store the name, address, phone number, and web address of each organization, group, or individual you find. Also identify the connection the organization, group, or individual has to your topic (supports research, interest group, treats patients, etc.). Create a report to summarize your findings. In Microsoft Word, create a letter that you can use to request additional information on your chosen organization, interest group, or individuals. Use the names and addresses in your database to merge with the letter. Select and then print the first two letters that result from the merge. Finally, write a paragraph describing what you learned about your topic that you previously did not know.

Job Study

City Improvement Projects

You work with the (fictitious) city council in your area to keep the public informed of the progress being made on improvement projects throughout the city. These projects are paid for through tax dollars voted on by the public, and the city council feels that keeping area residents informed will lead to good voter turnout when it is time to make more improvements.

Your job is to create a database and a table in the database that will store the following information for each project: a project ID number, a description of the project, the budgeted dollar amount to be spent, the amount of money spent so far, the amount of time allocated to the project, and the amount of time spent so far. Enter five city improvement projects into the table (using your own sample data). Create a query based on the table that calculates the percentage of budgeted dollars and the percentage of budgeted time spent so far. Print the table and the query.